# Cambridge Elements ≡

**Elements in Perception**
edited by
James T. Enns
*The University of British Columbia*

# THE EXPERTISE OF PERCEPTION

## *How Experience Changes the Way We See the World*

James W. Tanaka
*University of Victoria*

Victoria Philibert
*University of Toronto*

CAMBRIDGE
UNIVERSITY PRESS

# CAMBRIDGE
## UNIVERSITY PRESS

University Printing House, Cambridge CB2 8BS, United Kingdom

One Liberty Plaza, 20th Floor, New York, NY 10006, USA

477 Williamstown Road, Port Melbourne, VIC 3207, Australia

314–321, 3rd Floor, Plot 3, Splendor Forum, Jasola District Centre,
New Delhi – 110025, India

103 Penang Road, #05–06/07, Visioncrest Commercial, Singapore 238467

Cambridge University Press is part of the University of Cambridge.

It furthers the University's mission by disseminating knowledge in the pursuit of
education, learning, and research at the highest international levels of excellence.

www.cambridge.org
Information on this title: www.cambridge.org/9781108826419
DOI: 10.1017/9781108919616

First published 2022

*A catalogue record for this publication is available from the British Library.*

ISBN 978-1-108-82641-9 Paperback
ISSN 2515-0502 (online)
ISSN 2515-0499 (print)

# The Expertise of Perception

## How Experience Changes the Way We See the World

Elements in Perception

DOI: 10.1017/9781108919616
First published online: February 2022

James W. Tanaka
*University of Victoria*

Victoria Philibert
*University of Toronto*

**Author for correspondence:** James W. Tanaka, jtanaka@uvic.ca

**Abstract:** How does experience change the way we perceive the world? This Element explores the interaction between perception and experience by studying perceptual experts, people who specialize in recognizing objects such as birds, automobiles, and dogs. It proposes perceptual expertise promotes a downward shift in object recognition where experts recognize objects in their domain of expertise at a more specific level than novices. To support this claim, it examines the recognition abilities and brain mechanisms of real-world experts. It discusses the acquisition of expertise by tracing the cognitive and neural changes that occur as a novice becomes an expert through training and experience. Next, it looks "under the hood" of expertise and examines the perceptual features that experts bring to bear to facilitate their fast, accurate, and specific recognition. The final section considers the future of human expertise as deep learning models and artificial intelligence compete with human experts in medical diagnosis.

**Keywords:** perceptual expertise, vision, downward shift hypothesis, face recognition, the holistic hypothesis, cognitive neuroscience, convolutional neural networks (CNNs), artificial intelligence

ISBNs: 9781108826419 (PB), 9781108919616 (OC)
ISSNs: 2515-0502 (online), 2515-0499 (print)

# Contents

# 1 Introduction: How Experience Changes the Way We See the World

Experts see the world differently. On a walk in the woods, the bird expert immediately recognizes that feathery brown object flitting in the bush as a "chipping sparrow," while the same object appears to the untrained eye simply as a bird. The vehicle that comes roaring down the street is instantly identified as a "1964 Ford Mustang" by a car aficionado, whereas the novice sees the vehicle merely as some old noisy sports car.

Anecdotally, at least, it seems that experts perceive objects in their domain of expertise at a finer grain of visual detail and this is reflected in their ability to identify these objects with more specific, descriptive names. In this section, we try to unpack this interaction between perception, objects, and names. We will examine how experience changes the way we see things in our world and how the shift in perception is reflected in the category labels that we use to identify objects. By recognizing that the human mind employs categories at various levels of generality and specificity, we can notice that perceptual expertise is characterized by a *downward shift* in object recognition where experts move from a novice's broad classifications of everyday objects to a more detailed, what we will call subordinate level, for the objects in their domain of expertise.

Using the downward shift criterion, we examine the processes of real-world experts, such as expert birdwatchers and dog judges, as well as laboratory-trained experts. We will also consider the varieties and range of human experts such as children with defined special interests. We will consider the constraints and robustness of the expert recognition where it can be limited to the recognition of a single highly familiar object or extend to the recognition of novel unfamiliar objects in novel but related domains. Next, we will look under the hood of expertise and examine the kind of perceptual information (e.g., color, spatial frequency) that experts bring to bear to facilitate their expert recognition judgments. We then discuss changes in neural processes of object recognition as a consequence of domain-specific experience and trace the neural changes that occur as a novice becomes an expert. In the final section, we consider the future and fate of human expertise as deep learning models and artificial intelligence (AI) assist human experts in the realm of medical diagnosis.

## 2 The Basic Level Category As the Entry Point of Visual Recognition

Because a single object can be identified at multiple levels of abstraction, it is not obvious at what level the object should be instantiated, recognized, and named (Brown, 1958). My cat Max is a member of the general categories of "living thing," "animal," "mammal," but he is also a member of more specific categories such as the genus "Felis," the species "Chartreux," and even the specific category of his particular identity "Max." Because an object is simultaneously a member of many categories, the observer must decide the level at which the object is first identified and subsequently named. The name that I assign to the "furry creature" sitting on my couch is not arbitrary but reflects different kinds of perceptual and semantic information and reveals something fundamental about the underlying representations that govern the object recognition process.

In her seminal work, Eleanor Rosch (1976) argued that there is one preferred level of abstraction that takes precedence over all others – what she referred to as the "basic" level. This is the level of abstraction that defines the interactions between objects and humans in the environment. For Rosch, the basic level was defined by the "structure in the world" where object features form natural bundles of "perceptual and functional information that form natural discontinuities, and that basic cuts in categorization are made at these discontinuities" (Rosch et al., 1976).

To probe the contents of categories at different levels of abstraction, Rosch and colleagues employed a feature listing task where participants were asked to list characteristic features for objects at a general, superordinate level ("animal," "furniture," "vehicle"), an intermediate basic level ("bird," "chair," "car"), and a specific, subordinate level ("sparrow," "rocking chair," "sedan") of categorization (Rosch et al., 1976) (for a recent review, see Hajibayova, 2013). The key finding was that participants listed many more attributes for the basic categories than for superordinate categories and subordinate level categories. For example, participants described many more features for the basic level "car" (e.g., has four wheels, a steering wheel, can be electric or gas, has a trunk, has an engine, used to carry passengers) than the superordinate level "vehicle" (e.g., used for transportation) and the subordinate level "sedan" (e.g., four doors). Distinct from superordinate and subordinate level categories, participants can provide significantly more information about the appearance of a basic level object such as its parts and features (Rama Fiorini et al., 2014; Tversky, 1989; Tversky & Hemenway, 1984). In contrast, superordinate level categories contain abstract, semantic features (e.g., "animal": reproduces, breathes, is animated) and subordinate level categories contain detailed, perceptual features (e.g., "sparrow": small, brown, flits around).

According to Rosch, the basic level objects share a kind of "perceptual glue" that binds category members together in a way that category members start to look alike. For example, whereas members of the category "animal" (e.g., giraffes, beetles, and horses) vary considerably in their size and shape, members of the basic level category "dog" (e.g., beagles, boxers, and poodles) take on a similar visual appearance.

To demonstrate this idea, one study collected photographs of objects from a variety of superordinate categories such as furniture, clothing, vehicles, and animals (Rosch et al., 1976). After the photographs were standardized for size and orientation, they projected the objects onto a screen and traced the shape outlines of the objects on a piece of paper. The researchers then measured the amount of shape overlap for objects at different levels of categorization. Objects belonging to the same basic level category demonstrated a large amount of shape overlap indicating greater perceptual similarity at the basic level whereas objects from the different basic categories are dissimilar. For example, whereas all "dogs" roughly resemble one another in their visual appearance, dogs look different from members of contrasting basic categories, such as cats, horses, and rabbits (see Figure 1).

In contrast, objects belonging to the same superordinate level categories (animal, vehicle, furniture) displayed virtually no shape overlap. Conversely, subordinate level objects tend to share a great deal of shape overlap with other subordinate level category members and are therefore more difficult to perceptually differentiate. Thus, basic level categories constitute the optimum level for object recognition because, on one hand, category members are perceptually

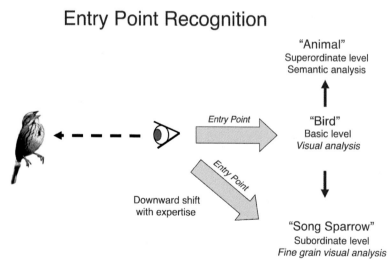

**Figure 1** An object can be classified at multiple levels of categorization. The entry point is the level of categorization at which an object is first recognized. For novices, the entry point is the basic level of categorization, and for experts, the entry point is the subordinate level.

similar to one another and, on the other hand, they are perceptually easy to differentiate from other contrasting basic level categories.

Given that objects are optimally differentiated at the basic level, it follows that people should show a basic level advantage in the speed of recognition or what has been referred to as the entry point of object recognition. The entry point is defined as the level of abstraction at which a perceived object stimulus *first* makes contact with an object representation in memory (Jolicoeur et al., 1984). In support of the claim that basic levels are the entry point of recognition is the fact that people typically prefer to use basic level terms such as "car," "chair," and "saw" when naming objects. This word preference suggests that this is the level that first comes to mind when identifying an object unlike more superordinate terms such as "vehicle," "furniture," or "tool" or more subordinate terms like "sedan" or "armchair" (Rosch et al., 1976).

Category verification tasks have been employed as a more exact measure of the speed of recognition. In this task, participants are shown a category label followed by a picture and are asked to decide whether the picture matches the category label. The consistent finding is that participants are fastest to verify objects with a basic level category label (e.g., "dog," "car") and slower to verify the same objects with a more general superordinate (e.g., "animal," "vehicle") or more specific, subordinate (e.g., "beagle," "Honda") label. These results provide compelling evidence that most people first recognize an object as a basic level category (Jolicoeur et al., 1984; Murphy & Smith, 1982; Rosch et al., 1976).

Category verifications that are superordinate or subordinate may take more time to process than the basic level verifications, but for different reasons. Members of the superordinate categories share abstract semantic properties that are not directly tied to the perceptual image of the object. For example, objects belonging to the superordinate category "animal" share features such that they "breathe," "reproduce," "are animate," and so on, but these characteristics are not "seeable" attributes but are more abstract related to an object's conceptual, semantic, and taxonomic properties. Consistent with this view, Jolicoeur et al. (1984) found that the time required to make superordinate categorizations ("animal") was the same regardless of whether participants were shown a basic level picture (e.g., dog) or a basic level word (e.g., "dog"). Hence, superordinate categorizations are not directly tied to the perceptual features of the object.

In contrast, subordinate level categories are inherently perceptual. For instance, to distinguish a warbler from a finch or to discern the difference between a meringue and a shitake mushroom, additional encoding time is needed to scrutinize the details of the object. As a test of the perceptual nature of subordinate level judgments, Jolicoeur et al. (1984) displayed pictures of common birds, dogs, cars, and boats for short (75 ms) and long durations (1,000 ms). Participants were asked to categorize the pictures at either the superordinate ("animal"), basic ("dog"), or subordinate ("collie") levels of abstraction. However, under the short exposure duration, participants were reliably slower and less accurate when categorizing objects at the subordinate level. The impaired performance indicates that additional encoding time was needed to abstract the perceptual details of the object when categorizing objects at the subordinate level.

For most of us, the basic level is the most immediate level at which the external perceptual object first makes contact with a stored representation in our visual memory. The primacy of the basic level category is reflected in our use of basic level words (e.g., "car," "dog," "tree") in language and language instruction. Basic level words are used the most frequently when adults converse with children (Callanan, 1985; Murphy, 2016), they are the words that children first use in language acquisition (Anglin, 1977; Bornstein & Arterberry, 2010), and they are the words that occur most frequently in written text (Wisniewski & Murphy, 1989). Thus, objects are optimally differentiated at the basic level in that objects that belong to the same basic categories are visually similar to one another and visually dissimilar to members of other basic level categories (Murphy & Brownell, 1985).

## 3 The Downward Shift Hypothesis

The story appears to be different for experts in their domain, however, where the most meaningful level of abstraction is the more specific, subordinate level. Because experts can employ a rich language of their own of many subordinate level terms, subordinate categories seem to be the most relevant and salient when investigating expertise. Veteran plumbers, for example, refer to a basic level wrench by its specific type such as a "basin," "chain pipe," or "monkey" wrench. Equestrians prefer to identify horses by their breeds, "Friesian," "Morgan," and "Arabian," or by the names of individual horses such as "Champ," "Bolt," or "Trigger." The language of experts reveals a more nuanced understanding and perception of objects in their domain of expertise that is more specific than the basic level of the novice. Anecdotally, at least, it seems that the experts are aware of the subtle, visual details that differentiate objects in their domain of expertise. A bird expert observes the characteristic markings, curved wings, and swooping movements of a barn swallow or the car expert appreciates the distinctive shape of the halogen, ringed headlight on a Series 3 BMW automobile.

The specific names used by experts, and their speed and accuracy, suggests a "downward shift" in their entry level recognition from the basic level to the subordinate level. Notably, in her original paper, Rosch observed that one of her participants – an airplane mechanic – seemed to perceive airplanes at a more specific level than the basic level applied by novices. For example, when making judgments about airplanes, this expert listed many more features than the other participants and could imagine airplanes from different perspectives. This expertise view posits that basic levels are not rigidly fixed by the perceptual structure of the world but are malleable to the influences of experience and learning. According to the downward shift hypothesis, with experience and learning, the entry level of recognition can shift to a level that is more specific and subordinate to the basic level.

To examine the "downward shift" claim, Tanaka and Taylor (1991) recruited expert dog judges and breeders and expert birdwatchers, all of whom had a minimum of ten years of experience in their specialty domain. Similar to the Rosch et al. (1976) study, the dog and bird experts were asked to perform a series of tasks (i.e., feature listing, naming, category verification) intended to tap into their entry level representations. Crucially, the bird and dog experts completed the entry level tasks for both bird and dog stimuli. In this design, the participants served as their own controls where they were expected to perform as experts when carrying out tasks in their domain of expertise (e.g., a bird expert naming pictures of birds) and behave as novices when performing tasks in the nonexpert domain (e.g., a bird expert naming pictures of dogs). Hence, these differences can be attributed to their experience rather than differences related to the participants themselves, such as their level of education, cognitive function, or motivation.

Following these methods, Tanaka and Taylor asked participants to list features for birds and dogs at the superordinate, basic, and subordinate levels. Consistent with Rosch's original findings, participants listed significantly many more features at the basic level than the superordinate or subordinate level in the novice domain. Critically, in their domain of expertise, participants added many more features at the subordinate level so that the subordinate categories contained as many distinctive features as the basic level. A large portion of these features were perceptual in nature, referring to the visual features such as color, size, and markings. For example, when listing features for the subordinate level "robin," the bird expert would note the distinctive eye-ring of the bird and its orange coloration. The feature listing task provides some evidence that experts view objects in their domain of expertise at a finer grain of analysis.

The type of label with which we spontaneously name an object provides insights into the level of the mental representation (Brown, 1958). As demonstrated by Rosch, for many of us, the most immediate level in naming is the basic level where we first identify an object by its basic level name ("chair," "car," "dog," "horse"). If experts are more attuned to the perceptual details that distinguish objects at the subordinate level, this increased distinctiveness might be reflected in preference for the subordinate level category in their naming behaviors.

In a free-naming study, Tanaka and Taylor presented pictures of common birds (e.g., robin, sparrow, cardinal) and dogs (e.g., beagle, German shepherd, poodle) to the expert participants and asked them to identify the images with the first name that comes to mind. Replicating the Rosch et al. (1976) results, participants produced basic level names the majority of the time (76 percent) when identifying objects in their novice domain. However, in their expert domain, participants were as likely to produce subordinate names as basic ones. The production of subordinate level names was more pronounced for bird experts, however, who used subordinates 74 percent of the time, compared to only 40 percent for dog experts. The naming difference between bird and dog experts might be due to the different demands of each expertise. Quick and accurate identification at the subordinate species level is what defines a bird expert whereas subordinate level naming is not as essential to the dog expert – many dog experts specialize in only one breed, for example. The naming results provide preliminary evidence that the subordinate level is the level that first comes to mind when experts of different domains identify objects.

If naming reflects the accessibility of subordinate level concepts, experts should also be fast to categorize objects at the subordinate level in a reaction time task. To measure the speed of recognition, Tanaka and Taylor (1991) used a category verification task where participants were asked to categorize pictures of objects from the expert and novice domains at either superordinate, basic, or subordinate levels as quickly as possible. When participants categorized objects in the novice domain (e.g., bird experts categorizing pictures of dogs), the results mirrored the original findings of Rosch et al. (1976) where participants were fastest to categorize objects at the basic level and slower at the superordinate and subordinate levels.

Interestingly, basic level response times in this study were the same for both expert and novice participants. For example, bird experts were as fast to categorize an object as a "dog" as dog experts, indicating that expertise has little effect on basic level judgments. However, a different pattern of results emerged when participants made subordinate level categorizations for objects in their domain of expertise. Consistent with the downward shift hypothesis, experts were as fast to categorize objects from their domain of expertise at the subordinate level as they were to categorize the same object at the basic level (see Figure 2). Although subordinate and basic level categorizations were equally accessible in terms of their reaction time responses, arguably subordinate level categories would be the preferred level of entry point recognition because they provide more attributes than basic level categories (e.g., we know more about an object if it is identified as a "robin" than as a "bird").

The Tanaka and Taylor (1991) experiments provide a plausible account of the downward shift hypothesis that expertise can alter the basic level. For the expert, perceptual knowledge of objects accumulates at the subordinate level, increasing the distinctiveness of this more specific category level (Murphy & Brownell 1985). This enhanced salience of subordinate level concepts allows the expert to spontaneously name and to quickly recognize objects at this specific level of abstraction. Based on these findings, experts perceive objects in their domain of expertise at a fundamentally different level of abstraction than the novices.

Results in favor of the downward shift hypothesis force researchers to reconsider what is meant by a basic level category. On one hand, Rosch et al. (1976) are correct that the structure of the world privileges a particular level of

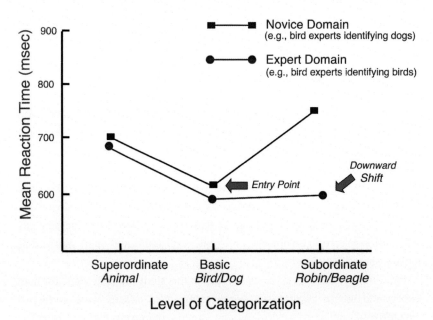

**Figure 2** Reaction time results from the Tanaka and Taylor (1991) study showing that experts demonstrate a downward shift in their entry point recognition where their response times are equally fast for subordinate level categorizations as basic level categorizations.

abstraction – the so-called basic level – where things begin to look alike. As a consequence, this is the level at which our knowledge about objects is concentrated. On the other hand, the basic level is not fixed by the external environment but is malleable to the influence of experience and motivation. As the expertise studies demonstrate, the so-called basic level can shift downwards to the more specific, subordinate level. For the expert, the subordinate level serves as their functional basic level in terms of where knowledge accumulates and how objects are recognized in their domain. The Rosch and expertise views can be reconciled by allowing for two types of basic level categories: a "structural" basic category that is predisposed by the perceptual environment and a "psychological" basic category that is defined by the intent and experience of the observer. For most of us when recognizing objects in our world, Rosch's basic level (e.g., car, chair, dog) is the most immediate and readily accessible representation based on the structure of things in the world and therefore serves as our entry point in recognition. However, for the expert, the subordinate level is the most salient and accessible category level at which domain objects are first named and recognized.

## 4 Everyday, Developmental, and Neurodivergent Expertise

Although only a fraction of the population qualifies as skilled birdwatchers or dog experts, people commonly perform acts of perceptual expertise in their everyday lives. We exhibit a downward shift in recognition when we quickly and accurately recognize the person coming down the hall as the face of our friend or colleague. Everyday perceptual expertise is demonstrated when we identify familiar places and buildings in our environment where common landmarks and monuments such as the Leaning Tower of Pisa are recognized faster at the instance level than at the basic level. Interestingly, familiar landmarks were slower to be categorized at the basic and superordinate levels than unfamiliar landmarks. For example, the familiar YMCA tower in Israel was slower to be verified as a "tower" than a nondescript unfamiliar tower (Anaki & Bentin, 2009). Similarly, people show a downward shift in recognition when they identify famous paintings by their name or by the particular artist's name (Belke et al., 2010).

Perceptual expertise is not only reserved for the identification of well-known pieces of art and architecture; expert recognition is exhibited every time we reach for our favorite coffee cup or put on our pair of cozy slippers. Miyakoshi et al. (2007) investigated this kind of personalized expertise by asking participants to passively view cups, shoes, handbags, and umbrellas that were their own personal items while monitoring their brain activity with

EEG. The results showed the brain response to personally familiar items was greater than to unfamiliar objects, suggesting that items previously known to participants were accessed through stored representations in visual memory. Pierce et al. (2011) found similar effects when participants identified their own personal items, such as their keys. Thus, unlike the expertise of birdwatchers, dog judges, and automobile aficionados, this type of personalized expertise is hyper-specialized, restricted to the recognition of a single item within the object category, and does not generalize to other category exemplars. For example, if a person is able to recognize their own golden retriever, their expert recognition does not necessarily transfer to the recognition of other golden retrievers.

In contrast to experts within a population, cross-cultural research has shown that groups of people or entire societies might demonstrate a level of recognition that is more specific than the conventional basic level. For example, Dougherty (1978) asked American children from an urban US city and Tzeltal Mayan children in Mexico to identify pictures of common plants. Whereas the US children labeled plants at the family level (e.g., tree), Tzeltal children labeled the plants by their more subordinate folk genera names (e.g., aspen, oak, redwood, and monkey tree). Why the difference in naming? According to Dougherty, the preferred level of categorization is determined by functional interactions between the environment and the categorizer. Because Tzeltal people live in an agrarian society, much of their lives revolves around their interactions with plants and knowledge about the local flora. For the Tzeltal, folk genera categories are the most efficient and informative level of abstraction in communicating plant knowledge. The cross-cultural work demonstrates that basic level categories are relative; what is basic to one culture is not necessarily basic to another depending on the category demands of the environment or culture (Malt, 1995; Winkler-Rhoades et al., 2010).

While it is not unusual for youngsters to become fascinated by a favorite toy, a particular pet, or the neighborhood construction tractor, for about a third of young children, this interest becomes more than a passing fascination but develops into an "extremely intense interest" (EII) (DeLoache et al., 2007). Like adult experts, the EII children are obsessed with things from their domain of interest and seek out opportunities to pursue and engage in activities related to their passion. One such child exhibited an extreme interest in trains:

> [F]rom about 18 months of age, he would point out anything that resembled train tracks – car tracks in the sand at the beach, fences, stitching on clothing, and even zippers. After he received a Thomas the Tank Engine railroad set for his second birthday, he played with it for hours every day. He even slept with his trains. He watched train videos that his parents and others bought for him

"countless times." The local librarian knew of his interest and saved books about trains for him to check out on his weekly visit.

(DeLoache et al., 2007, p. 1582)

EII typically emerges at about eighteen months of age, is three times more prevalent in boys than girls (Alexander et al., 2008; DeLoache et al., 2007), and is positively correlated with scores on verbal intelligence tests (Johnson & Eilers, 1998; Johnson & Mervis, 1994). Children with EII are enamored with items from more conventional categories such as automobiles, dinosaurs, and trains, but they can also become obsessed with things from more idiosyncratic object domains such as blenders, puzzles, or *Wizard of Oz* memorabilia (Alexander et al., 2008; DeLoache et al., 2007). For the child with an EII, the interest is relatively long-lived (lasting at least sixteen to twenty-two months), exhibited in different social contexts (home, friends' homes, school), directed toward multiple objects/activities within the category of interest (real objects, replicas, pictures, videos, social media), and frequently noticed by people outside the immediate family (friends, extended family, teachers) (DeLoache et al., 2007).

Like adult experts, children with EII demonstrate a downward shift in their recognition strategies in which they prefer to identify objects in their domain of interest with subordinate level rather than basic level labels (Johnson & Eilers, 1998; Johnson et al., 2004; Johnson & Mervis, 1997). For example, "Ari" at two years of age developed an EII for birds and birdwatching (Johnson & Mervis, 1994). By age 4 years 5 months, Ari was able to identify 118 different types of perching birds. Similar to adult experts, Ari's expertise involved a sophisticated understanding about the taxonomic relations and behavioral habits of birds. To test his conceptual knowledge, Ari was presented with a triad of birds and asked which two "go together." Unlike his age-matched novice peers who made their groupings based on perceptual features, Ari sorted his birds based on nonvisual conceptual features (like diet or habitat).

Although children with EIIs possess an integrated, coherent knowledge about domain objects that allow them to go beyond their obvious explicit perceptual features to uncover their implicit functional connections (Gobbo & Chi, 1986), other research suggests that they are not mini-adult experts. When conceptual knowledge and perceptual appearance are pitted against one another, children with EII, unlike adults, will rely more on visual-based explanations, indicating that a child's deeper theory about objects can be overridden by their surface features (Johnson et al., 2004). Whereas the conceptual knowledge of expert adults is flexible and robust, the knowledge of children with EII is more compartmentalized and restricted to the domain of interest. For example, when drawing inferences about dinosaurs, both child and adult experts were able to make inferences about familiar dinosaurs. For instance, both groups correctly inferred that the long neck of the Mamenchisaurus dinosaur allowed the animal to eat leaves from tall trees. However, adult experts were able to apply causal concepts to novel domains, such as shorebirds, where the adults were able to infer that the long toes of the Gallinule shorebird helped to support its weight on water plants (Johnson et al., 2004). In contrast, children who possess extensive knowledge about dinosaurs were not able to make inferential leaps to shorebirds. In sum, children with EII demonstrate unusual abilities to recognize and make inferences about objects in their domain of interest. At the same time, the inferential judgments of EII children were more strongly bound to the perceptual appearance of objects and restricted to their specialized domain of interest.

As outlined by the *Diagnostic and Statistical Manual of Mental Disorders – Fourth Edition* (DSM-IV), children on the autism spectrum are characterized by repetitive and restricted behaviors. For some children on the spectrum, restricted behaviors manifest themselves as perseverative and stereotypic motor movements (e.g., rocking back-and-forth movements), but for others, these restricted behaviors are displayed as circumscribed interests in specific domains that are not dissimilar to the interests exhibited by children with EII. However, in contrast to children with EII, children on the autism spectrum become so absorbed and consumed by their circumscribed interest that it comes at a cost of establishing meaningful social relationships with others (Klin et al., 2007).

Circumscribed interests are exhibited in 90 percent of surveyed children on the autism spectrum and often appear by preschool ages (Klin et al., 2007). The circumscribed interests of children on the autism spectrum include the same domains typical of children with EII with a focus on nonsocial domains, such as mechanical objects, trains, rocks, cartoon characters, calendars, Pokémon, and dress-up clothing (Klin et al., 2007; Turner-Brown et al., 2011). As an indicator of their expertise, autistic children with circumscribed interests display a downward shift in identification for objects in their specialty domain. For example, a child with a circumscribed interest in Pokémon identified these characters with specific subordinate level names (Grelotti et al., 2005).

Although spanning a range and diversity of interests, it has been speculated that the common factor of circumscribed activities in autism is the identification of patterns in stimuli –what some have referred to as "systemizing" (Baron-Cohen et al. 2009; Baron-Cohen & Wheelwright, 1999). Systemizing is the motivation to analyze and understand the regularities and rules that govern a system in order to predict how that system will behave. Systemizing can take on many forms, such as motion systemizing (e.g., watching washing machines), spatial systemizing (e.g., obsession with maps and routes), and mechanical systemizing (e.g., obsession with vacuum cleaners). The precursor to systemizing theory is the child's hyper-attention to the perceptual details of the system that comprise its basic rules or features (Baron-Cohen et al., 2009; Wang et al., 2007). For children with circumscribed interests, attention to detail is an important step for achieving an understanding of the workings of the complete system (Baron-Cohen et al., 2009).

In summary, children with EII and autistic children with circumscribed interests share some similarities with adult experts. Like adult experts, children with special interests attend to the perceptual details of the stimuli (Baron-Cohen et al., 2009) and exhibit a downward shift when identifying objects in their domain (Grelotti et al., 2005; Johnson & Mervis, 1994; Johnson & Eilers, 1998; Johnson et al., 2004). Like adult experts, the perceptual and semantic advantages of children with specialized interests appear to be confined to familiar objects and categories in their domain. So, while EII and autistic children present many of the trademark characteristics associated with perceptual expertise, they often lack the deeper conceptual knowledge that are the standards in adult expertise.

## 5 Perceptual Expertise in the Laboratory

Studying experts "in the wild" provides valuable insights into the consequence of real-world expertise; however, these studies fall short of explaining the *process* by which a person acquires perceptual expertise. For this reason, laboratory training studies are helpful for understanding the conditions and mechanisms that produce expertise (Gauthier & Tarr, 1997b; Scott et al., 2008; Tanaka et al., 2005). In a standard laboratory training study, researchers have full control over the selection of participants, the training stimuli, the schedule, and the monitoring of training performance and the learning and transfer conditions (Shen et al., 2014). However, the tradeoff of laboratory studies is their ecological validity; that is, by tightly controlling participant, stimulus, and learning factors, these studies might miss the richness and nuances of expertise as it is acquired and occurs in the real world.

Based on the abovementioned studies of real-world experts, we know that one hallmark of perceptual expertise is a downward shift in their entry level recognition to a much more detailed perceptual representation as reflected in the accessibility of the subordinate level word labels. Can subordinate level labels be "reversed engineered" to promote perceptual expertise? Can the same linguistic labels be applied to induce fine-grain visual perceptions in the laboratory? In a landmark study, Gauthier and Tarr (1997) designed families of artificial "yoda-like" objects that they referred to as "Greebles." Like natural categories, Greebles who belong to the same family shared basic level features in that they all contained the same parts (boges, quiff, dunth) arranged in a similar configuration (see Figure 3). Hence, learning to identify Greebles at the subordinate level required detailed detection of subtle variations in the Greeble parts and configuration. In their training experiment, participants learned to identify the Greebles at the different levels of categorization: family (samar, osmit, galii), sex (plok, glik), and individual (pimo) based on Greeble parts (boges, quiff, dunth).

Over the course of two weeks, participants received ten sessions of training to classify the Greebles at the family, sex, and individual levels. After training, participants demonstrated the characteristic downward shift in recognition where their response times to identify the Greebles at the individual level approximated the response times to identify the Greebles at the more general family and gender levels. Moreover, expert participants were faster to identify Greebles whose boges, quiff, and dunth parts were arranged in a similar configuration as the trained Greebles than Greebles shown in a new configuration. The sensitivity to the configuration of parts was found in experts but not in novices. Whereas learning generalized to new Greebles with similar parts and configurations as the training Greebles, the learning did not transfer to Greebles with new parts and configurations. The transfer results suggest that perceptual expertise was fine-tuned to specific types of Greebles and the configuration of parts but did not generalize to new families of Greebles.

Another important question is whether it is the *quality* or the *quantity* of the perceptual training that drives expertise. Experts invest countless hours engaged

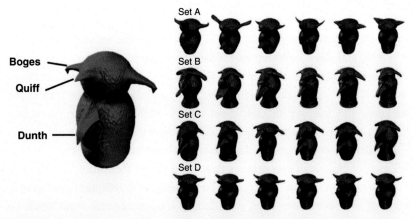

**Figure 3** Examples of Greeble parts and Greeble families (Gauthier & Tarr, 1997a).

in activities related to their avocation; birders go on birdwatching field trips, car aficionados attend car shows, and trainspotters spend hours observing trains. It is plausible that experts simply have more perceptual exposure to and experience with objects in their domain of expertise than novices and this experience leads to the downward shift effect.

As a test of the quantity versus quality accounts of perceptual expertise, Tanaka et al. (2005) taught novice participants to classify ten varieties of wading birds and ten varieties of owls at either the subordinate species level (e.g., "great blue crown heron," "eastern screech owl") or the family level of abstraction ("wading bird," "owl"). During training, the amount of visual exposure was such that participants received an equal number of learning trials for wading birds and owls; the only difference was that one family of birds was categorized at the species level (e.g., "green heron") and the other birds at the family level (e.g., "owl"). Pre- and post-training performance was measured in a same or different discrimination task in which participants judged whether pairs of bird stimuli belonged to the same or different species.

The key finding was that participants trained in species-level discrimination conditions recognized trained and novel exemplars learned at the species level, but no transfer was found of exemplars learned at the family level. Thus, perceptual categorization, not perceptual exposure or experience per se, is important for the development and generalization of visual expertise. The importance of subordinate labeling in expertise training has been replicated for learning geometric objects (Wong et al., 2009), cars (Scott et al., 2008), birds (Scott et al., 2006), and other-race faces (Lebrecht et al., 2009; Tanaka & Pierce, 2009). In studies of real-world experts, the subordinate level terms are the products of perceptual expertise indicating a downward shift in recognition. In studies of laboratory-trained experts, subordinate level terms serve as the linguistic "hooks" that orient the observer to a more specific level of visual analysis that creates the downward shift (for an example of label-less subordinate level learning, see Bukach et al., 2012).

The value of laboratory studies is that expert recognition can be "reversed engineered," such that predicted variables mediating perceptual expertise can be isolated, controlled, and tested. However, a shortcoming of the perceptual training approach is that lab experts do not possess the rich knowledge that real-word experts bring to bear in their recognition. For example, the accomplished birder knows that in a wooded forest habitat they are more likely to see certain species of birds (e.g., flycatchers, tanagers, nuthatches) and this top-down knowledge helps to constrain the range of options in object recognition. For real-world experts, domain-specific semantic knowledge is essential in expert car recognition (Barton et al., 2009; Dennett et al., 2012; McGugin et al., 2012) and expert bird recognition (Johnson & Mervis, 1997; Tanaka & Taylor, 1991).

It is obvious that experts know more about the objects in their domain of expertise than novices – after all, they are experts – but it is less obvious how their conceptual knowledge might influence their perception of objects in their domain of expertise. To address this question Boster and Johnson (1989) asked sport fishing experts and novices to rate the relative similarity of different pairs of sporting fish such as black sea bass, red snapper, and smooth puffer.

Novices who had little background knowledge of sporting fish based their judgments on perceptual properties, such as the shape of fins (e.g., "both had continuous fins across the top") or body type (e.g., "both fish had long and skinny bodies"). Experts, on the other hand, gave not only perceptual explanations like these but also conceptual explanations for their similarity decisions, such as "both fish are caught in the surf during the summertime." Interestingly, the similarity judgments of the fishing experts were more variable than the judgments of novices. Having had extensive personal experience and knowledge of fish, the experts were more likely to be idiosyncratic in their similarity decisions. For example, Expert A might know the specific details about a particular species of fish that is less familiar to Expert B, whereas Expert B might know fish species unfamiliar to Expert A. The differences in their conceptual knowledge and experience contributed to the variability in their similarity judgments.

Although a mechanic, a car salesperson, and a vintage collector might share a passion for automobiles, their expertise of cars will be expressed in different ways. The seasoned mechanic knows how to change a carburetor or replace a fan belt, the salesperson knows the features and prices of the latest makes and models of cars, and the vintage car buff knows about the historical facts of classic automobiles. Thus, the same object category recruits different varieties of perceptual and functional knowledge depending on the specialty of the expert and the task demands required for their expertise.

To demonstrate this point, Medin et al. (1997) examined the category knowledge of three types of tree experts: taxonomists, landscape workers, and park maintenance personnel. They found that taxonomists and maintenance workers identified different perceptual properties of trees, whereas landscape workers differed from the other two types of experts with respect to the functional properties associated with trees. Although all three types of expertise required specialized knowledge of trees, the kind of knowledge needed to fulfill the pragmatics of that expertise differed across the groups. Despite sharing the same domain (i.e., trees or fish), there are considerable group differences in their knowledge of the domain and substantial intragroup differences depending on the experiences of the experts. Collectively, these studies indicate that not all experts are created alike – that even within an expert domain there is much diversity. How a perceptual expert "sees" an object in their domain of expertise will depend on the kind of knowledge that they possess about the objects and the goal of their interactions with the objects.

## 6 Cognitive Mechanisms: Attention, Encoding, and Short-Term Memory

Imagine this scenario. You and your friend are out shopping at the local mall on a busy weekend. The parking garage is packed with cars, but you manage to find a spot. At the end of your shopping excursion, you return to the parking garage only to realize that you forgot exactly where you parked your car. Sadly, as you stare out at the sea of cars, you realize that your compact-sized, Japanese automobile resembles almost every other vehicle in the lot. Fortunately, your friend, a car salesperson, happens to be familiar with the particular make, model, and year of your vehicle. Your friend makes a quick scan of the parking garage and immediately spots your car parked in a nearby stall.

*Visual Search.* Scenes are visually rich stimuli containing a multitude of objects broadly distributed across the visual field, with each object varying in its size, shape, and color. To locate a particular object in a scene, the visual system cannot simultaneously attend to all objects but must examine each object individually, one at a time. An important question is whether experience and familiarity with the objects sought can influence the speed at which they can be found in a visual search.

To address this issue, Hershler and Hochstein (2009) asked car and bird experts to identify a target car or bird object in a visual array containing a variety of objects such as chairs, balls, shoes, and toys. In this visual search task, they found that experts were reliably faster to detect objects in their domain of expertise than objects outside their expert domain. That is, bird experts were faster to find bird targets than car targets, whereas car experts showed the opposite search advantage for car targets over bird targets. Because both experts were given the same test arrays, their faster reaction times were not due to any features of the stimuli but to the prior knowledge and familiarity with objects in their domain of expertise.

To better understand the expert's search advantage, Hershler and Hochstein (2009) created a salience map in which the reaction times were displayed as a function of their spatial location in the visual array. For example, the upper left-hand corner of the saliency map represented the reaction time of a target item when it appeared in the upper left-hand corner of the search array. When participants searched for objects close to the fixation point, not surprisingly, their search times were fast and accurate. Critically, when targets were located in the periphery, the experts showed only a slight increase in their detection times for objects in their domain of expertise as shown in red in Figure 4. However, when participants were searching for objects *outside* their domain of expertise, detection time increased as the target locations moved into the periphery as shown in blue in Figure 4. Based on this evidence, the authors suggested that, for objects in their domain of expertise, experts formed templates that helped guide the search processes across a broader spatial area, efficiently separating the potential target images from the nontarget images.

If object templates can facilitate performance when they are the targets of a visual search, would these same templates hinder performance when objects of expertise are irrelevant distractors? To address this question McGugin et al. (2011) recruited car experts and novices and asked them to search for target faces in an array that contained distractor images of cars. For novices, the car distractors had little effect on the pattern of their search behaviors compared to their search times for control stimuli (i.e., photos of sofas). However, for the experts, there was an interference effect where they were slower than novices to find the target faces when they were shown among car distractors. Interestingly, the magnitude of the interference effect correlated with independent measures of car expertise such that the best experts tended to show the strongest interference effects.

The visual search studies suggest that the observer's ability to detect objects in a complex scene can be fine-tuned by experience and top-down knowledge. On the positive side, experts are faster to locate objects in their domain of expertise across a broader region of the search space using object templates (Hershler & Hochstein, 2009). However, on the negative side, experts are distracted by the presence of expert objects even when the images are not relevant to the search task at hand. Thus, it is plausible that the expert object templates that facilitate performance when they are the targets of visual search are the same templates that automatically draw attention and impair performance when they are the nontarget distractors of visual search.

*Visual Encoding.* As a defining characteristic of their perceptual expertise, experts are faster to make subordinate level categorizations of objects in their domain of expertise than novices (Johnson & Mervis, 1997; Tanaka & Taylor, 1991). However, because there are multiple steps in the recognition processes involving perceptual encoding, categorization, decision-making, and motor response, the source of the expert recognition advantage is not obvious. That is, experts may be more efficient in extracting diagnostic information from a stimulus or they might also be better at accessing the right subordinate level representation or even in

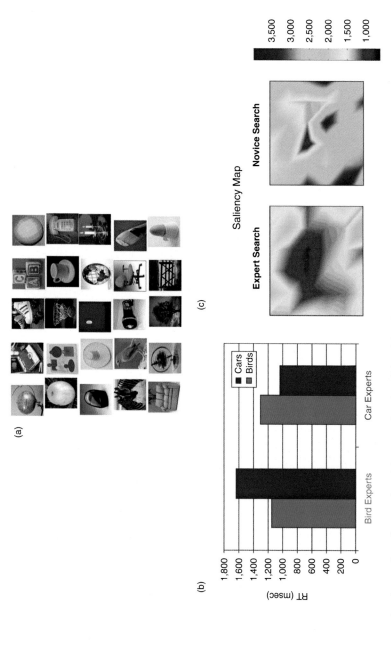

**Figure 4** Visual search and expertise: (a) example stimuli used in visual search task with bird and car experts; (b) average reaction time of bird and car experts searching for car and bird targets; (c) saliency map showing reaction times for targets presented in the central and peripheral areas of the display; red indicates faster response times and blue indicates slower response times (Hershler & Hochstein (2009).

executing a speeded motor response. Any or all of these factors would contribute to an expert's ability to classify an object at the subordinate level.

In an important study, Curby and Gauthier (2009) tested whether expertise affects the visual encoding early in recognition. In their study, participants were presented with a car stimulus for either 12, 47, 82, 118, 153, 235, 494, or 1000 ms followed by a second car stimulus. The participant's task was to decide whether the first and second car stimuli were the same or different models of cars. For the "same" trials, the car stimuli belonged to the same category of car type but could differ in superficial image properties, such as shading and luminance. The investigators found that in exposure durations as brief as 48 ms the car experts performed above chance levels, indicating that the influence of their top-down expertise knowledge was evident at this early stage of perceptual processing. In contrast, car novices required 118 ms of encoding time to achieve the same level of performance (see Figure 5). While discrimination ($d'$) performance of both expert and novice groups improved at a similar rate with increased exposure duration time, the peak asymptote for experts was much higher than the level achieved by novices, indicating that, despite the additional viewing time, novices lacked the perceptual knowledge to make accurate discrimination judgments. These results indicate one source of the expert's recognition advantage occurs at the earliest stage of object recognition and involves the rapid encoding of diagnostic features of objects in the domain of expertise.

*Visual Short-Term Memory.* Visual short-term memory (VSTM) is a temporary memory buffer where a limited number of items can be stored to support an ongoing cognitive task. On average, people can hold about three or four visual items in their VSTM (Vogel et al., 2001). However, the capacity of VSTM is not fixed and can vary with object complexity. Specially, it has been shown that visually complex objects, such as shaded cubes, placed greater demands on VSTM than simpler objects like letters and uniformly colored squares, reducing its overall capacity (Alvarez & Cavanagh, 2004).

The capacity of VSTM is not rigidly fixed but can be influenced by the experiences of the observer. Specifically, familiar objects require less processing than less familiar objects. Faces are a good example of complex, but highly familiar objects. Curby and Gauthier (2009) demonstrated that people show a larger VSTM capacity for upright faces that is greater than the capacity for cars, watches, and inverted faces. In a follow-up study, Curby et al. (2009) showed the capacity of VSTM was increased for highly familiar objects of expertise. They found that car experts showed a larger VSTM capacity for cars compared to novices and, critically, the expert advantage was eliminated when the car stimuli were inverted.

(a)

(b)

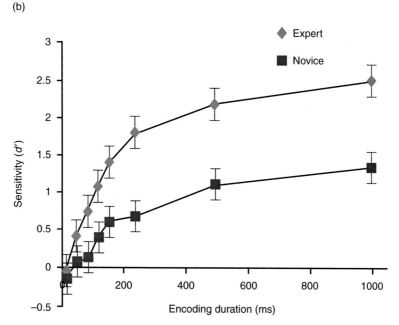

**Figure 5** The sensitivity (*d'*) of car experts and car novices in making "same/different" discrimination decisions and encoding duration (Curby & Gauthier, 2010).

Based on this evidence, they speculated that car expertise relies on holistic processing and this process is disabled when the car stimuli are turned upside down. According to object-based theories of VSTM capacity, holistic encoding may allow experts to integrate the multiple features of a car into the unified object representations, thereby reducing the memory load of VSTM (but, for an alternative view, see Scolari et al., 2008).

As the foregoing studies demonstrate, real-world and laboratory-trained experts are quick, accurate, and specific when identifying objects in their domain of expertise. In terms of their cognitive behaviors, experts are faster to find expert objects during a visual search (Hershler & Hochstein 2009), are faster to recognize expert objects under brief exposure conditions (Curby & Gauthier 2009), and have a greater VSTM memory capacity for objects of expertise (Curby et al. 2009).

## 7 Face Recognition and the Holistic Hypothesis

Although the foregoing research studies characterize the cognitive behaviors of a perceptual expert, they do not directly address the mental representations that mediate these behaviors. That is, what is the nature of the representation that drives the expert's perceptual advantage in subordinate level recognition, visual search, and short-term memory? In this section, we explore the diagnostic information (e.g., color, spatial frequency, motion) that experts employ to facilitate the very fast identifications in their domain of specialization. We start by comparing the processes of object expertise to another type of expertise that virtually all of us possess: our expertise with faces.

A common claim is that most people are *face experts* who can recognize familiar faces, such as those of celebrities like Brad Pitt, Beyoncé, Meghan Markle, and Taylor Swift, quickly, accurately, and at subordinate levels of abstraction (Barragan-Jason et al., 2012). Indeed, face recognition constitutes the most specific type of subordinate level recognition of individuation where each face serves as its own unique category by being frequently identified with a proper name label (e.g., Bob, Susan, Javon) (Tanaka, 2001). At the basic level, all faces share a perceptual similarity, such that all faces possess the same features (i.e., eyes, nose, mouth) placed in the same general configuration (i.e., the eyes are above the nose, which is above the mouth). Therefore, one face can only be individuated from another face by detecting relatively subtle variations in the shape of its features and their configuration. Despite the perceptual demands imposed by individuation, most people are "experts" in face recognition and can recognize a familiar face accurately, quickly, and with little cognitive effort.

What are the processes underlying our face recognition expertise? Given the structural similarity of faces, it has been speculated that faces are recognized not on the basis of a single feature but on the ensemble of facial features that are fused together to form an integrated whole – an operation that has been referred to as holistic processing. According to the holistic hypothesis, holistic processing emerges when (1) the individuated objects are structurally similar to one another, (2) they require quick and accurate discrimination, and (3) the subjects have sufficient experience to be sensitive to the structural properties that individuate category members.

Most forms of perceptual expertise satisfy the requirements for holistic processing. After years of experience and practice, experts have honed their ability to quickly and accurately recognize objects in their domain of expertise at subordinate levels of abstraction. Therefore, it seems reasonable to expect that perceptual experts would demonstrate evidence of holistic processing when recognizing objects in their domain of expertise. In the face recognition literature, three measures – the inversion task, the parts-and-wholes task, and the composite task – have served as the benchmarks of testing holistic face processing. In the expertise literature, these same tasks have been applied to assess whether holistic processes are found in expert recognition.

*The Inversion Test.* While most objects are more difficult to identify when turned upside down, faces seem to be *disproportionately* impaired by inversion relative to the recognition of other objects – the face inversion effect (Yin, 1969). According to holistic accounts, when a face is inverted, holistic processes are disrupted, forcing the observer to perceive the face not as an integrated whole but in terms of its individual parts thereby impairing face recognition (Rossion, 2008). A strength of the inversion manipulation is that the visual properties of the face stimulus (e.g., luminance, contrast, spatial frequency) are preserved in an upside-down face, yet people are slower and less accurate to identify an inverted face, suggesting that inversion selectively disrupts a face-specific process.

To probe for an expert inversion effect, Diamond and Carey (1986) recruited expert dog judges and tested their recognition for breeds of dogs presented in their upright and inverted orientations. Critically, a reliable inversion effect was obtained when the judges made recognition judgments for canine breeds within their area of specialization, but no inversion effect was found for the dog breeds that were outside of their breed of specialization. Consistent with the holistic expertise hypothesis, the authors speculated that the dog judges employed holistic processes for individuating dogs by their breed of specialization and, consequently, recognition judgments were vulnerable to the effects of inversion. However, when identifying breeds outside of their realm of expertise, they utilized a more analytic, or piecemeal, strategy as evidenced by the lack of an inversion effect.

Since Diamond and Carey's study, evidence for the holistic expertise hypothesis has been mixed. The majority of expertise studies have shown that inversion does not necessarily affect the accuracy of expert recognition, but it can slow the speed of recognition, as was the case for handwriting (Bruyer &

Crispeels, 1992), fingerprints (Busey & Vanderkolk, 2005), Greebles (Gauthier et al. 1998; Gauthier & Tarr, 1997b) and cars and birds (Gauthier et al., 2000; B. Rossion & Curran, 2010). That recognition can be slowed by inversion indicates that while access to holistic processes may be impeded by inversion, it is not completely abolished.

In an attempt to replicate the original Diamond and Carey (1986) results, Robbins and McKone (2007) tested Labrador dog judges and breeders for their recognition of faces and dogs presented in their upright and inverted orientations. Contrary to the Diamond and Carey study, they found that the inversion effect for the dog experts was comparable (upright: 70 percent versus inverted: 62 percent) to the inversion effect obtained for the age-matched novices (upright: 64 percent versus inverted: 60 percent). Moreover, the magnitude of the dog inversion effect for the experts was smaller (8 percent) than that inversion effect obtained for faces (17 percent). Because the inversion effect increased only slightly with experience and did not approach the size of the face inversion effect, they concluded that expert recognition does recruit holistic processes.

However, the Robbins and McKone study fell short of providing a definite test of the holistic expertise hypothesis. Specifically, the expert breeders and judges selected for their study specialized in British-type Labradors, but more than half (thirty-eight of the sixty) of the stimuli depicted the visually dissimilar American-type Labradors. Thus, the mismatch between test stimuli used in the experiment and the domain of expertise of the participants might explain why the expert participants performed no better than the novice participants in the recognition of upright dogs (Robbins & McKone, 2007).

A variant of the holistic expertise hypothesis was recently evaluated by Campbell and Tanaka (2018) in which they tested the recognition abilities of budgerigar breeders. Budgerigar breeders are passionate hobbyists who keep between 50 and 500 birds in their aviaries. Although the birds are not typically named, the breeders claim that they are able to individuate each bird with respect to its age, sex, personality characteristics, and genetic lineage. Similar to faces, birds share basic features and markings that appear in similar spatial arrangements (see Figure 7). Thus, given the number of birds raised by the breeders and their ability to individuate their birds, budgerigar expertise provides the ideal domain for testing the claims of the holistic expertise hypothesis.

Campbell and Tanaka (2018) tested budgerigar experts and age-matched novices for their recognition of upright and inverted budgerigars and faces. They found that novices showed a robust inversion effect for faces but their overall recognition of budgerigars was poor. Further, there was no difference in recognition between upright and inverted budgerigars. Budgerigar experts did not differ from novices on the face recognition task but were superior to the novices in their recognition of budgerigars, thereby validating their expertise. Critically, the experts demonstrated a robust inversion effect for budgerigars and the magnitude of the inversion effect was comparable for faces.

Although the expert inversion results are consistent with the holistic expertise hypothesis, a limitation of the inversion paradigm is that the source of the inversion effect is not specified. Whereas inversion disproportionately disrupts the recognition of faces and objects of expertise, it is not clear whether holistic processes are selectively impaired by misorientation. In the face recognition literature, the composite task and the parts-and-wholes task are designed to directly test for the presence and absence of holistic processing.

*Composite Task.* In face processing, a compelling demonstration of holistic face processing is the face composite task (Young et al., 1987). In this paradigm, a composite face stimulus is created by aligning the top half of one face with the bottom half of another (as shown in Figure 6). This manipulation produces the impression of a new composite face identity with neither the top half nor the bottom half of the face resembling the original identity of the person depicted. In the face composite test, participants are instructed to attend to

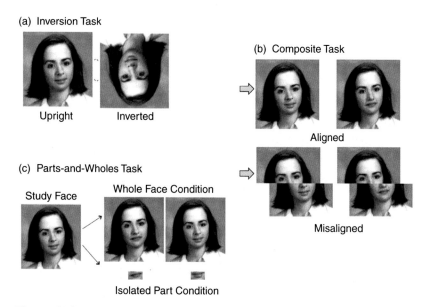

**Figure 6** Three tests of holistic processing: (a) *inversion task* – participants are tested for their recognition of upright and inverted faces; (b) *composite task* – participants are instructed to attend to the top half and ignore the bottom half as indicated by the arrow cue; (c) *parts-and-wholes task* – participants learn a study face and are then asked to select the correct mouth from the study face.

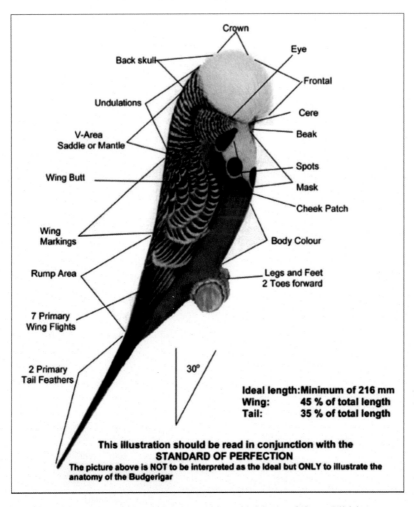

**Figure 7** Illustration of the common markings of the exhibition
budgerigar (Campbell & Tanaka, 2018).

and identify the person according to the top (or bottom) half of the face and to
ignore information in the other half of the face (see Figure 8). However, owing
to holistic interference, participants find it difficult to decouple the two face
halves from each other, as reflected in their slower response times and lower
accuracy rates. Critically, when the face halves are misaligned or the composite
face is inverted, the holistic interference effect is attenuated (Young et al.,
1987), thereby disrupting the holistic illusion (Rossion, 2013).

Are experts susceptible to holistic interference? Gauthier et al. (2003) investigated interference in the expert holistic processing of cars and faces. In their
study, car experts and car novices were asked to make same/different judgments

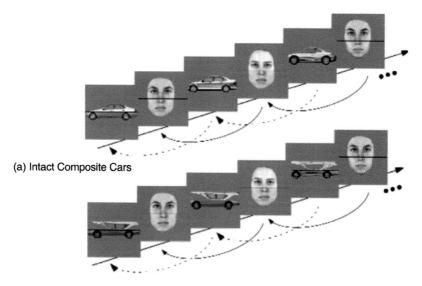

(a) Intact Composite Cars

(b) Inverted Composite Cars

**Figure 8** Two-back interleaved part-matching task designed to measure holistic processing for cars and for faces (Gauthier et al., 2003). Composite faces and cars were interleaved in either (a) an intact (familiar) or (b) transformed (tops inverted) configuration (Gauthier et al. 2003).

based on the bottom halves of alternating composite face and car images. Their results showed that the magnitude of the holistic car interference effect was correlated with self-reports; the more experienced car experts exhibited a stronger inference effect. Interestingly, the amount of interference for cars was correlated with the magnitude of interferences for faces. One interpretation of this finding was that the mechanism used for expert recognition must be similar to the mechanism applied for faces.

Composite tasks have since been used to demonstrate interference in other expert domains involving holistic perception, such as fingerprints (Busey & Vanderkolk, 2005), X-rays (Bilalić et al., 2014), musical notation (Wong & Gauthier, 2010), and chess boards (Bilalić et al., 2011). Composite interference effects have been demonstrated during the perception of English words (Wong et al., 2011), Portuguese words (Ventura et al., 2017; Ventura et al., 2020), and Chinese characters (Wong et al., 2011), suggesting holistic processes are used in reading.

While holistic processes have been shown in real-world experts, training studies have also demonstrated that holistic processing emerges as a consequence of training with artificial objects (Greebles: Gauthier & Tarr, 1997; Ziggerins: Wong et al., 2009). One study trained two groups of participants to rapidly classify thirty-six artificial objects (Ziggerins) either at the subordinate level of the name or at the basic family level (see Figure 9). Behaviorally, the participants who learned to individuate Ziggerin showed the classic downward shift in producing speeded subordinate level classifications and these participants exhibited an increase in their holistic processing on the composite task after learning. In contrast, the basic level participants showed an improvement in their basic level categorizations and displayed no changes in their holistic processing. The Ziggerin results show that holistic processes are recruited when participants are trained to differentiate structurally similar objects at subordinate levels of categorization but not when those same objects are learned at the basic level. Hence, it is not the *quantity* of perceptual experience that promotes holistic processing but the *quality* of the experience as dictated by the task demands of expertise. In the Wong et al. (2009) study, both groups of participants were exposed to the Ziggerin objects an equal number of times, but only the subordinate group showed evidence of holistic processing.

*Parts-and-Wholes Task.* In the face recognition field, the parts-and-wholes task has been employed to directly measure the holistic representation of faces. In this paradigm, participants learn a series of faces (e.g., Joe, Bob, Fred) and then their memory for specific parts is tested. Memory for the parts is tested either when shown in isolation or when shown in the context of the whole face. In the whole face test condition, the target and foil faces are identical with the exception of the critical part under examination. As shown in the example in Figure 3, recognition for Brad Pitt's nose is tested in a whole face in which the eyes and mouth are kept constant in the target and foil faces. Critically, then, in

**Figure 9** Examples of Ziggerin objects shown in their object families (Wong et al., 2009).

the whole face and isolate part test conditions, the target and foil items only differ with respect to the critical feature under testing. However, if memory for the individual features of a face is integrated into the whole face representation, recognition of the face part should be better when presented in the whole face context than when tested in isolation. Consistent with this prediction, part recognition was superior when presented in the context of the whole face (Tanaka & Farah, 1993). However, no evidence of holistic recognition was found when the studied and test stimuli were scrambled faces, non-face stimuli (houses), or inverted faces. In these cases, the recognition of the individual part did not benefit from the context of the whole stimulus forcing an analytic approach to encoding (Tanaka & Farah, 1993). Based on this evidence, it has been argued that faces are represented as unified, non-decomposable forms where part and configural information are integrated as a *holistic* face representation (see also Donnelly & Davidoff, 1999).

The holistic expertise account predicts a similar whole object advantage when experts are identifying parts of objects from their domain of expertise. In an unpublished study, Tanaka et al. (1996) tested the holistic recognition of three types of real-world experts: cell biologists, car buffs, and Rottweiler dog breeders.

Expert participants had at least five years' experience and were currently active in their field of specialization. Biological expertise was chosen as a suitable comparison domain because biological cells, similar to faces, have identifiable parts (i.e., nucleus, nucleus, mitochondria) that can be manipulated in the frontal plane. Although the configuration of the cell parts varies, biology experts learn to differentiate different cell types based on the shape and spatial differences between the parts. Car expertise was a plausible test domain given that automobiles have discernible features (e.g., headlights, grill, bumper) that are arranged in a prototypical configuration. Finally, experts who specialize in the breeding and judging of Rottweiler dogs were also investigated for the parts-and-wholes study. However, in contrast to previous studies where experts were tested for their recognition of dogs shown in profile (Diamond & Carey, 1986; Robbins & McKone, 2007), Tanaka and colleagues measured the ability of their experts to recognize the frontal facial features of the dogs. It is typical for dog experts to be sensitive to the facial characteristics of their dogs because facial composition is taken into account when judging the overall quality of the animal. In this study, experts were asked to identify parts from their domain expertise displayed in isolation or in the whole expert object using the parts-and-wholes task.

Surprisingly, all three kinds of experts showed no evidence of holistic processing in their respective domains of expertise relative to the novices. Both experts and novices showed evidence of holistic processing where recognition was better when the part was tested in the whole object than when tested in isolation. The absence indicates that holistic recognition is not necessarily exclusive to expert recognition but can be applied in situations of nonexpert recognition. In this study, it was informative that the cell, car, and dog experts fared no better in their recognition of expert objects than novices. The lack of an expert/novice difference shows that experimental stimuli in the parts-and-wholes task failed to capture the critical qualities of perceptual expertise from these domains. For the biologists, holistic processing might be less essential because the configuration of parts contained within a cell vary in their spatial arrangement, thereby inducing a more part-based strategy. To test car and dog expertise, previous studies have depicted car (Gauthier et al., 2003) and dog (Diamond & Carey, 1986) stimuli in full profile, whereas the car and dog stimuli used in the parts-and-wholes task depicted only the frontal portions of the cars and dogs. It is possible that stimuli displayed in these formats do not tap into the perceptual skills necessary for the expertise in recognizing these types of objects.

According to the holistic hypothesis of expertise, holistic processing is required for the rapid identification of expert objects at subordinate levels of abstraction. Results from the inversion task show that, like face experts, real-world object experts exhibit a robust inversion effect for objects of expertise (Busey & Vanderkolk, 2005; Campbell & Tanaka, 2018; Chin et al. 2017; Diamond & Carey, 1986; Gauthier et al., 1999; Rossion & Curran, 2010). Similarly, results from the composite task reveal that experts exhibited holistic inference when they are asked to selectively attend to one portion of an expert object while ignoring the other (Gauthier et al., 2003). Compatible with holistic expertise view, participants show evidence of holistic processing after subordinate level training, suggesting that holistic processing facilitates the rapid recognition associated with perceptual expertise (Gauthier & Tarr, 1997; Wong et al., 2009.) However, contrary to the holistic expertise position, the cell, car, and dog experts failed to show a holistic advantage on the parts-and-wholes task. Taken collectively, the empirical evidence indicates that the fast, subordinate level recognition of perceptual expertise is mediated by a degree of holistic processing. However, this is not to say that holistic recognition is the only route to expertise. Other research discussed in the following section has indicated that a blend of global and local strategies facilitate the expert's keen ability to recognize objects in their domain of specialization.

## 8 Global and Local Processing

In his classic field guide to birdwatching, the illustrator Roger Tory Peterson employed two graphical techniques to highlight the types of information that are useful in bird identification. In the first technique, displayed birds in silhouettes show the basic shape outlines of each taxonomic family level (Peterson, 1998). As shown in Figure 10, birds can be discriminated at this level based solely on their size and shape information, absent any internal features. At a finer grain of categorization, Peterson used arrows to highlight the features that differentiate similar species of birds or to show within-species developmental or sex differences. For example, the immature orchard oriole can be discriminated from its adult version based on its black throat patch and Bullock's oriole is identifiable from other orioles according to its distinctive eye-ring. Peterson's method suggests that bird recognition requires the encoding of the external shape of the bird as well as attending to visual features that distinguish birds at the species level.

Perceptual expertise involves attending to the *global* shape outline of an object as well as attending to its internal *local* details. When diagnosing a radiological image, for example, the expert radiologist makes an initial scan of the X-ray image to determine whether it is "cancerous" or "noncancerous" (Kundel & Nodine, 1975; Swensson, 1980). This assessment can be accomplished very quickly in exposure times as brief as 250 ms (Evans et al., 2013). Guided by general information in the initial scan, the radiologist then engages in a more deliberate "search and find" mode to localize the specific site of the lesion and to assess its abnormality. In contrast to the global-to-local shift that accompanies radiological expertise, the less experienced radiologist engages in the slower and less accurate "search-to-find" mode (Krupinski & Jiang, 2008). In this model, the detection and localization phases are distinct but interdependent operations where the global phase of detection constrains the search conducted in the localization phase of identification.

However, Evans et al. (2013; 2016) offered an alternative account in which they argued that the detection and localization stages involved in radiological

**Figure 10** Families of common birds differentiated by silhouette.

assessment are executed independently of one another. According to their account, the initial scan signals information about the status of the image (cancerous or noncancerous) but does not contain information about its specific location if cancerous. To support this claim, Evans et al. (2013) presented expert radiologists and novices with brief presentations of bilateral mammograms. Half of the mammogram stimuli were normal images and the other half contained a subtle mass and architectural distortion of varying sizes (10–48 mm). If participants detected an abnormality in the image, they were asked to indicate its location on a blank mammogram with a mouse click. Mouse clicks falling within an area determined by the ratio of the lesion area and overall tissue area were considered as correct responses.

The key finding was that the detection rates of expert radiologists were above chance levels at the brief exposure duration of 500 ms; however, their localization decisions were outside the boundaries of the lesion. According to Evans et al. (2013), 500 ms was sufficient time to extract a "gist" signal about the normality of the mammogram but not enough time to extract information about its location (but see Carrigan et al., 2018). While experts might make expert decisions in a "blink of an eye," they might not be consciously aware of the reasons for their decisions.

## 9 Diagnostic Features: Color and Spatial Frequency

In this section, we explore how the expert's knowledge about the diagnostic features of an object influences their ability to make fast, precise identifications at fine levels of discrimination.

An essential requirement for perceptual expertise is knowing the diagnostic features of an object; that is, what are the characteristics that differentiate one object from another. The expert mushroom hunter is aware of the features that differentiate a *Macrolepiota rachodes* mushroom from its close neighbor the *Macrolepiota procera* mushroom, and the veteran trainspotter can visually distinguish a General Electric Dash 8-40 C from a General Electric C44-9 W with ease. However, the diagnostic features required for expert recognition are not always evident. What is considered a perceptual feature to one person is not necessarily regarded as one by another.

In a study by Biederman and Shiffrar (1987), novice participants were asked to categorize pictures of one-day-old chicks as male or female. Because the diagnostic cues necessary for this category task were not obvious, participants performed at chance levels even when provided with feedback. However, after the participants were told the location and shape of the critical feature, accuracy improved to expert levels. The chicken sexing findings highlight the distinction between what the casual observer sees as a perceptual feature and what the expert views as a diagnostic feature. Although an observer might be aware of an object's perceptual features, they might not be aware of its diagnostic utility with respect to identification and categorization (Schyns, 1998; Schyns & Rodet, 1997).

However, knowing the diagnostic features of a category is no guarantee that it will improve diagnostic performance. For example, in dermatology training, students are taught the diagnostic features of skin cancer using the ABCDE rules representing five salient features of a lesion regarding its asymmetrical shape (A), irregular border (B), variegated color (C), a size that is greater than 6 mm in diameter (D), and evolving appearance (E). If a lesion meets ABCDE diagnostic criteria it is suspicious and the patient is referred to a dermatologist for further evaluation.

Unfortunately, training programs based on the ABCDE diagnostic guidelines have not been successful with medical practitioners whether they are nurses (Oliveria et al., 2001), medical students (Aldridge et al., 2012), or primary care physicians (Chen et al., 2001). In the case of melanoma, adopting a featural approach to diagnosis is problematic for two reasons. First, participants (e.g., primary care physicians, laypersons) might not have the necessary diagnostic skill to detect the presence of a diagnostic feature or might have a tendency to misclassify a noncancerous lesion as melanoma. Second, melanoma and benign lesions represent "fuzzy" categories whose features are not exclusive and ruled-based but more probabilistic and overlapping (Ashby & O'Brien, 2005). Fuzzy categories are acquired best when learners have extensive experience classifying a broad range of category examples and are provided with feedback on their category decisions (Ashby & Ell, 2001; Roads et al., 2018; Xu et al., 2016).

## Color

In vision, color plays a critical role in the early stages and the later stages of object processing. In the early stages, color helps to segment the object from its background information and to delineate the internal part features of the object (Gegenfurtner & Rieger, 2000). In the later stages, color knowledge is integrated into the object representation. There are stronger color associations for some objects than others. For example, apples are red, bananas are yellow, and alligators are green. For other objects, especially human crafted ones, color assignments seem less systematic and more arbitrary where a car can be blue or red or a hat can be green or yellow. In object recognition research, objects with strong color associations are said to be "high" in *color diagnosticity*, whereas objects that are either weakly associated with color or lack color associations are regarded as "low" in color diagnosticity (Tanaka & Presnell, 1999).

Although early models of object processing have minimized the contributions of color (and texture) to recognition (Biederman & Ju, 1988), subsequent studies have shown that color affects object recognition across different tasks such as naming and category verification (Bramão et al., 2011; Martinez-Cuitino & Vivas, 2019; Rossion & Pourtois, 2004). Color is also influenced by object category (natural versus human-made) (Nagai & Yokosawa, 2003), provides a valuable cue under suboptimal viewing conditions (Tanaka & Presnell, 1999; Wurm et al., 1993), and influences our perceptions in other sense modalities (Spence et al., 2010). Thus, for things that we recognize in the world, color matters.

Is color important in expert recognition? The domain of birdwatching seems ideally suited to explore this question. As objects of recognition, the color provides useful clues to the identities of birds. Veteran birdwatchers know that birds can vary in color depending on the time of year and the age and gender of the bird. Bird identification requires quick and accurate recognition of birds that are often structurally similar in their global shape and, therefore, color would be a valuable secondary source of information to aid in their discriminations. As an indication of their color knowledge, experienced birdwatchers were more likely than novices to list color attributes that describe birds at the subordinate level, indicating that color knowledge is employed in feature listing tasks (Tanaka & Taylor, 1991).

A 2014 study tested the role of color in veteran birdwatchers and novices (Hagen et al., 2014). In the experiment, bird experts and novices were asked to recognize familiar birds shown in their congruent color, an incongruent color, or grayscale at either the subordinate family level (e.g., hummingbird, woodpecker, sparrow) or the species level (e.g., Tennessee warbler, Wilson's warbler). Both bird experts and bird novices demonstrated a congruency effect in which the congruently colored birds were recognized faster than incongruently colored birds (see Figure 11). Interestingly, response time distribution analysis revealed color effects were observed at different times for the two groups. For the novices, color effects were found at the slower reaction times, suggesting that color knowledge was accessed later in the recognition process. In contrast, the experts demonstrated an advantage for congruent colored birds at their fastest responses and this advantage was maintained across all response intervals. These results suggest that the experts apply their color knowledge quickly and automatically, whereas color knowledge is accessed more slowly and more deliberately by novices.

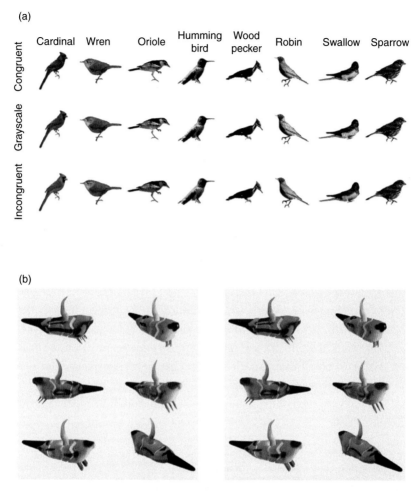

**Figure 11** The effects of color on object recognition: (a) common birds shown in their congruent colors, grayscale, and incongruent colors; (b) artificial stimuli (Sheinbugs) shown in congruent colors and grayscale (Hagen et al., 2014).

To test the functional role of color in subordinate level expertise learning, Devillez et al. (2019) taught participants to categorize finches or warblers at the subordinate species level and at the more general family level. Training images were presented in their natural colors across six sessions. Before training, any color helped performance, but color congruence effects (congruent > incongruent) only emerged after subordinate level training and congruency effects were maintained, even when tested a week later.

These results complement the findings with real-world bird experts showing that novices integrate color information into their object representations during the acquisition of subordinate level concepts. An overall color effect was found in a training study with artificial objects called Sheinbugs. Here, participants learned one family of full-color, artificial objects at the subordinate (species) level and another full-color family at the basic (family) level (Jones et al., 2018). After learning, their subordinate and basic level recognition was tested with color and grayscale images. A color advantage was observed in both the basic level and the subordinate learning conditions, suggesting that color can be a useful diagnostic cue at the multiple levels of categorization.

## Spatial Frequency

Spatial frequency (SF) analysis is a useful technique for separating the global shape and fine-grain information in an image. As shown in Figure 12, fine variations in luminance contained in high spatial frequencies (HSFs) reflect the internal details and edges of an object. By comparison, coarser luminance variations captured by low spatial frequencies (LSFs) represent an object's global form (Morrison & Schyns, 2001). In visual processing, different ranges of the SF spectrum have been shown to be critical for the recognition of letters (Solomon & Pelli, 1994), line drawings and geometric silhouettes (3 to 6 cycles per object: Braje et al., 1995), and faces (8 to 16 cycles per face: Costen et al., 1994, 1996). In object categorization, subordinate level classification of non-face objects relies more heavily on HSFs (~16 cycles per object) relative to basic level classification of the same objects (Collin & McMullen, 2005; Harel & Bentin, 2009).

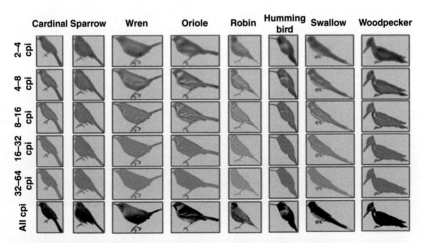

**Figure 12** The effects of spatial frequency (SF) on object recognition. Common birds whose spatial frequencies contain 2–4 cycles per image (CPI), 4–8 CPI, 8–16 CPI, 16–32 CPI, 32–64 CPI, and all spatial frequencies (Hagen et al. 2016).

To test the influence of SF on expertise, expert birdwatchers and novices were asked to identify common birds (e.g., robin, cardinal) that were bandpass filtered to isolated specific SF ranges and masked with the bird's contour (Hagen et al., 2016). This combined manipulation preserved the bird's global form while systematically degrading its internal feature information (see Figure 12). Consistent with previous work (Hagen et al., 2014; Tanaka & Taylor, 1991), bird experts were more accurate and faster at recognizing birds at the family level than novices. Experts and novices recognized the images best when presented in the mid-SF range (8–16 cycles per image) than the LSF range (<8 cycles per image) and HSF range (>16 cycles per image). The reaction time patterns showed that the experts, but not the novices, utilized the mid-range SF information to facilitate their fast recognition times.

In a training study with artificial objects, it was also shown that images containing information in the 8–16 cycles per image range produced the best results for the recognition of subordinate level objects (Jones et al., 2018). Interestingly, the mid-range frequencies (i.e., 8–16 cycles per image; e.g., Costen et al., 1994, 1996) have been shown to be the optimum SF range in face recognition. It has been claimed that mid-range SF are optimal for high-lighting the details of the internal features of an object while conveying con-figural information (Goffaux et al., 2005), information that is vital for face recognition and for expert recognition.

## 10 Neural Substrates: EEGs and the N170 Component

We have argued that the behavioral benchmark of perceptual expertise is a downward shift in recognition where the expert is as quick and as accurate to recognize objects in their domain of expertise at the subordinate levels as they are to recognize objects at the basic level. The expertise research shows that the preferred level of human object recognition is not fixed but is malleable, shaped by the observer's experience and the demands of their environment. The behavioral evidence suggests that differences observed between experts and novices should be reflected in differences in their neural processes.

In this section, we examine group differences in the brain activity of extant experts and novices as well as trace changes in brain activity as a novice becomes an expert. First, we examine EEG studies that record the temporal dynamics of perceptual expertise at the millisecond-by-millisecond timescale. Next, we review the functional magnetic resonance imaging (fMRI) studies that compare the metabolic brain activity of experts to novices in neural structures implicated in expert processes. Collectively, the electrophysiological and neuroimaging methodologies provide a window into the brain processes mediating the "when" and "where" of perceptual expertise.

## EEG: The Temporal Dynamics of Perceptual Expertise

Electroencephalography (EEG) is a neuroscientific method in which electrical activity from the brain is recorded noninvasively by electrodes placed on the scalp of the participant's head. In event-related potential responses (ERPs), this electrophysiological activity is time-locked to the onset of an external stimulus such as a sound or picture. While a single ERP trial is inherently noisy due to the weak brain signals and recording artifacts, when many stimulus trials are averaged together, prototypical brain wave patterns (i.e., ERP components) emerge from the brain data that reflect specific cognitive processes (Luck, 2014).

One such component is the face N170. Research has shown that when participants view faces these stimuli elicit an early negative ERP component in the right temporal electrode channels approximately 170 ms after the onset of the face stimulus. The magnitude of the N170 component is significantly larger in response to faces than other natural and human-made objects like cars, dogs, or flowers (for a comprehensive review, see Rossion & Jacques, 2011). Thus, relatively early on in neural processing, the brain activity elicited by faces is differentiated from the brain activity elicited from non-face objects. Importantly, the privileged processing of faces cannot be attributed to its unique low-level properties (e.g., SF, contrast, luminance) because when face stimuli are turned upside down the N170 component is significantly reduced or delayed.

A long-standing question in the ERP face processing literature is whether the enhanced N170 potential is specific to faces or whether this component generalizes to other objects of expertise. To investigate this question, Tanaka and Curran (2001) monitored bird and dog experts while they categorized images of common birds and dogs. In their design, participants served as their own controls in that they were expected to perform as experts when categorizing objects in their domain of expertise but were expected to respond like novices when objects were outside of their domain. According to the face-specific hypothesis, if the enhanced N170 is unique to faces, then expertise would be expected to have little influence on this early ERP component. In contrast, if the N170 can be modulated by experience, the expertise hypothesis predicts that experts demonstrate an enhanced N170 component but only when viewing objects from their domain.

Consistent with the expertise hypothesis, experts showed a greater N170 component when viewing expert objects within their domain of expertise and a reduced N170 when viewing objects outside of their domain of expertise (see

Figure 13). Because the bird experts demonstrated a larger N170 component to bird stimuli and dog experts demonstrated a larger N170 component for dog stimuli, the N170 expertise effect cannot be attributed to properties of stimuli but to the experience and abilities of the observer. The Expert N170 has been demonstrated in training studies where participants were trained to individuate artificial objects, such as "blobs" (Curran et al., 2002), Greebles (Rossion et al., 2002; Rossion et al., 2004), Japanese characters (Maurer et al., 2008), and Chinese characters (Fan et al., 2015).

The Tanaka and Curran (2001) results suggest that the enhanced N170 component reflects a domain-general process of expert recognition rather than a process that is specific to face recognition. What is not clear is whether the Expert N170 uses a holistic process for face recognition. Measuring the ERPs of fingerprint experts is the ideal test for addressing this question because they identify individual fingerprints based on their characteristic ridge patterns,

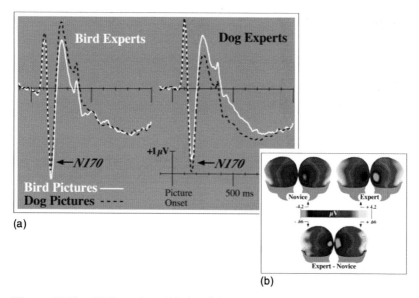

**Figure 13** The EEG results of bird and dog experts showing the N170 effect: (a) wave plots of the composite N170 channels for bird experts (left) and dog experts (right) – for each group, event-related potentials (ERPs) are plotted separately for bird and dog stimuli; (b) topographic distribution of the N170 expertise effect. The illustrations at the top show mean voltages from 140 to 188 ms after picture onset separately for novice and expert domains. The illustration at the bottom shows mean voltage differences between expert and novice domains between 140 and 188 ms after picture onset (Tanaka & Curran 2001).

swirls, bifurcations, texture, and pore positions in a canonical upright orientation with the finger pointing up. If holistic processes are employed in expert
fingerprint identification, these processes should be impaired when fingerprints
are turned upside down.

To test this prediction, Busey and Vanderkolk (2005) recorded the ERPs of
fingerprint experts and novices while viewing faces and fingerprints. Both
experts and novices showed an increased and delayed N170 to inverted faces,
which was not surprising given that both groups were face experts with years of
experience in recognizing faces. Despite this, the brain activity of the expert and
novice groups was very different when presented with upright and inverted

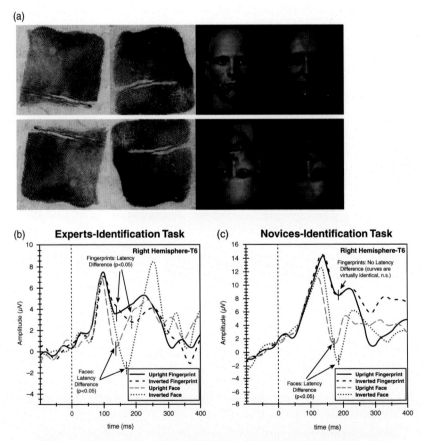

**Figure 14** Recognition of upright and inverted faces and fingerprints
by experts and novices: (a) examples of upright and inverted fingerprint and
face stimuli; (b) the ERP waveforms of experts to upright and inverted
fingerprints and faces; (c) the ERP waveforms of novices to upright and inverted
fingerprints and faces (Busey & Vanderkolk 2005).

images of fingerprints. Whereas the novices showed no differences in their ERPs to upright and inverted fingerprints, experts showed a delayed and greater N170 response to inverted fingerprints compared to upright fingerprints (see Figure 14). In other words, the fingerprint experts showed the same delayed and increased N170 ERP activity to inverted fingerprints that people show to inverted faces. Busey and Vanderkolk's (2005) findings reinforce two important points about the N170 component and perceptual expertise. First, it is a general marker of perceptual expertise in specific category domains (e.g., faces, dogs, birds, fingerprints); second, it is a neural index of holistic process that is disrupted when objects of expertise (faces or fingerprints) are turned upside down.

The ERP results indicate expert object recognition and face recognition processes engage common cognitive processes and neural mechanisms (Gauthier et al., 2000). Based on the interference effect, it is plausible that the neural processes engaged in expert object recognition and face recognition would compete with one another. To test the interference claim, Gauthier et al. (2003) employed a composite task where car experts and novices were presented with interleaved composites of faces and cars. Participants were instructed to attend only to the bottom half of the objects and to decide whether the bottom part matched that of the last object of the same category. In the holistic condition, normal cars and normal faces were interspersed with normal intact cars. In the non-holistic expert condition, normal cars were interspersed with cars with their tops turned upside down. Behaviorally, car experts demonstrated holistic interference where it was more difficult for experts to attend to the bottom portion of the car when it formed a normally looking vehicle than when the top was inverted.

With respect to the EEG data, the magnitude of the Expert N170 correlated with behavioral measures of performance where the best car experts showed the greatest reaction. Critically, when the cars were interleaved with faces, the face N170 was significantly reduced, suggesting a competition effect between face recognition and expert object recognition processes. That is, the neural resources allocated for face recognition were depleted by the concurrent demands imposed by expert car recognition.

As a direct test of face and expert object competition, one study presented cars and faces to car experts and novices (Rossion et al., 2007). The images were presented either simultaneously or with the face presentation trailing by 200 ms. When presented simultaneously, the magnitude of the N170 to faces was significantly reduced, suggesting that car and face processes were competing for the same cognitive resources. However, when the presentation of the face was delayed by 200 ms, the magnitude of the face N170 was reinstated, suggesting that the slight delay was sufficient for the car processes not to interfere with face processes. Thus, the collective ERP evidence on the Expert N170 makes several key points: (1) the N170 is a not a face selective component but is reserved for processing of all expert objects; (2) the N170 is linked to holistic processing used in the recognition of expert objects; (3) expert object and face recognition converge on a common neural mechanism and compete for resources when processed concurrently.

Whereas the occipital-temporal N170 ERP is responsive to the basic level categories of expertise (e.g., faces, birds, cars), a later component, the N250, has been associated with within-category, subordinate level distinctions, such as recognition of celebrity or personally familiar faces (Huang et al., 2017; Schweinberger et al., 2004; Tanaka et al., 2006; Wiese et al., 2018). To separate the basic level N170 and the N250 components in expert object recognition, Scott and colleagues recorded ERPs of the participants to images of wading birds and owls. They then trained participants to classify wading birds and owls at either the basic or the subordinate level (Scott et al., 2006). Critically, the number of learning trials was equivalent in the two training conditions, such that participants were presented with an equal number of owl and wading bird images, and only differed with respect to the level at which the images were classified. After six days of training, participants displayed an enhanced N170 response to the owl and wading bird images relative to their pre-training levels. Interestingly, the magnitude of the N170 response was the same regardless of whether participants learned to classify the birds at the basic or subordinate levels. Hence, the N170 reflects the amount of category exposure or experience to exemplars, irrespective of the level at which the exemplars were first categorized (Scott et al., 2008). As a perceptual component, the N170 reflects the extensive visual experiences of experts who seek out every opportunity to view objects in their domain of expertise.

In contrast to the N170, the N250 component was sensitive to the level of category training. Participants demonstrated a greater N250 to the bird family used in subordinate level training but not to the bird family used in basic level training. The post-training N250 also generalized to new images of trained species and new species within the subordinate level family. For example, participants who learned to make subordinate level categorizations to owls (e.g., great gray owls, burrowing owls, barred owls) demonstrated an N250 response to novel owl images not used in training and to owl images from untrained but related species. The robustness of the N250 component suggests that prior expert category knowledge provides the scaffolding for acquiring new, related subordinate categories.

As an alternative to the event-related methods in EEG, Rossion and colleagues have applied the method known as fast periodic visual stimulation (FPVS) to study the processes of object and face processing (Liu-Shuang et al. 2014). FPVS employs an adaptation technique in which a sequence of stimuli is rapidly presented at a fixed interval (i.e., base stimulus) and, within the sequence, a stimulus from another category is presented (i.e., oddball stimulus). The magnitude of the brain's response to the oddball stimulus provides an index of category discrimination. Applying FPVS, Hagen and Tanaka (2019) recorded EEG activity while bird experts and novices viewed a sequence of "base" bird images from the same family (e.g., robin) or species (e.g., sparrow) presented at a frequency of 6 Hz (i.e., 6 images per second). Every fifth stimulus was an "oddball" image depicting a different family-level bird (e.g., warbler) or species-level bird (chipping sparrow) occurring at a frequency of 1.2 Hz (i.e., about once every 83 ms). As the comparison expertise category, face stimuli of the same identity (e.g., Sam) were presented at 6 Hz base frequency and a face stimulus of a different identity (e.g., Fred) was presented at 1.2 Hz oddball frequency (see Figure 15a). The results showed that, for experts, the magnitude of the oddball response for species-level birds and faces was strongly correlated. In contrast, the novices demonstrated a relatively weak correlation between their response to species-level oddball and the face oddball (see Figure 16b). These findings suggest that experts tap into the same neural resources when making within-category discriminations for birds as they use when making within-category discriminations for faces.

Whereas EEG methodologies are well suited to pinpoint the "when" of perceptual expertise, fMRI provides a snapshot about the "where" of perceptual expertise, that is, identifying the brain structures that are differentially engaged when experts view objects of expertise. In fMRI, it is assumed that cognitive operations increase the hemodynamic activity, referred to as their blood oxygen level–dependent (BOLD) response, in localized brain areas (Glover, 2011). The BOLD response is captured by fMRI techniques at spatial resolutions as precise as 0.8 cubic mm (Margalit et al., 2020). This fine-grain spatial resolution comes at the cost of its temporal resolution where hemodynamic response is delayed (one data point is normally obtained within 1–2 s), which is significantly slower than the millisecond timing afforded by EEG methods.

In investigating perceptual expertise, researchers compare the BOLD response of real-world experts and novices in order to understand how the brains of experts might differ from the brains of novices. In a seminal study, Gauthier and colleagues recruited bird and car experts and showed them images

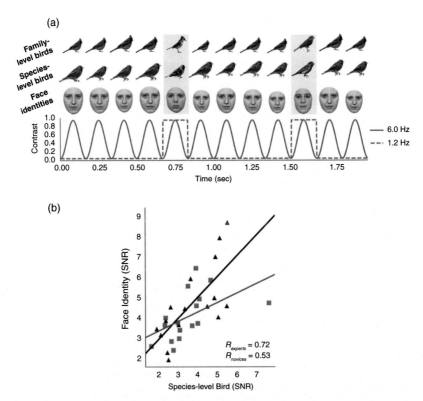

**Figure 15** The fast periodic visual stimulation (FPVS) methodology:
(a) bird or face images are presented at the base frequency of 6.0 Hz
(i.e., 6 times per second) – a different face or bird identity is presented at an
oddball frequency of 1.2 Hz (i.e., 1.2 times per second); (b) the magnitude
of the signal-to-noise (SNR) response to the oddball face and oddball
species bird was more strongly correlated for experts (triangles) than
novices (squares) (Hagen & Tanaka 2019).

of faces, familiar objects, cars, and birds while they were in an fMRI scanner. As
expected, when viewing faces, the experts exhibited heightened brain activation
in the right fusiform face area (FFA) relative to the activation elicited by object
stimuli (Gauthier et al., 1999). In the FFA, the experts exhibited a selective brain
response to objects in their domain of expertise that was stronger than the
response to control objects but was only slightly weaker than the response to
faces. The expertise response was category selective such that bird experts
showed an increased BOLD response to birds, whereas car experts exhibited
enhanced brain activity to cars. Gauthier and colleagues' results provide compelling evidence that FFA activation was driven by the participant's area of

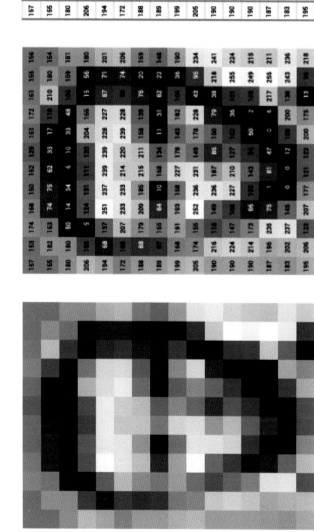

**Figure 16** An image of Abraham Lincoln can be represented as a matrix of pixel values. Note the spatial contingencies in the image where adjacent pixels are likely to share similar luminance values.

expertise, not by a particular set of visual properties associated with the object category, such as birds are more curvilinear and cars are more rectilinear in shape.

A plausible explanation of the expertise results was that the experts were responding to face-like properties contained in the expert stimuli. On this view, bird experts were responding to the bird *faces* and car experts were responding to the face-like configuration of symmetrical headlights ("eyes") and the grill ("mouth") (Kanwisher, 2000). To test this possibility, Xu (2005) reduced the "facedness" characteristics of the stimuli by showing side-view photographs of birds and cars to experts. Despite reducing the face qualities of the stimuli, Xu found that experts demonstrated a robust FFA activation to objects in their domain of expertise that was correlated with perceptual expertise performance.

Subsequently, researchers have reported robust FFA activity in other category domains such as medical diagnosis (Bilalić et al., 2016; Harley et al., 2009) and chess (Bilalić et al., 2011). In developmental populations, young children with EII and children on the autism spectrum exhibited a heightened FFA response to objects in their specialty domains (Gomez et al., 2019; Grelotti et al., 2005; James & James, 2013). In the Greeble training study, participants showed a higher fMRI response in the right FFA for matching upright "Greebles" than for inverted "Greebles" (Gauthier & Tarr, 1997; Gauthier et al., 1998). Rather than being exclusively dedicated to the recognition of faces, the expertise findings reveal that FFA shows remarkable plasticity whose function can be used in expert recognition.

Other neural structures besides the FFA have been implicated in perceptual expertise. Harel et al. (2010) tested car experts and novices while they were monitored for repeated images of cars or airplanes. In the high expertise engagement condition, experts were asked to respond to cars and to ignore the airplane stimuli. When the cars were the relevant category of response, the experts exhibited enhanced BOLD activation in the FFA that extended to the early visual areas and the parahippocampal place area (PPA), showing that the effect of perceptual expertise was spread across multiple brain areas. Other studies have shown that perceptual experience recruits medial fusiform gyrus, lingual gyrus, and precuneus brain areas (McGugin et al., 2012). However, in the "low expertise engagement" condition, where experts were asked to respond to airplanes and to ignore the car stimuli, brain activity in expertise-related brain regions (FFA, PPA, early visual areas) was significantly reduced and similar to the activity elicited by cars in novices. Hence, the expert brain areas are not automatically activated by the presence of expert stimuli but are engaged when they are important to a given task.

In summary, perceptual expertise produces brain changes in the fusiform gyrus of real-world experts (Gauthier et al. 2000), laboratory-trained experts (Gauthier et al. 1999), and young children with special interests (Grelotti et al. 2005; Gomez et al. 2019; James & James 2013). Studies employing electrophysiological methods have shown that the N170 and N250 brain components that are commonly associated with face processing are activated during expert recognition. Thus, similar to faces, objects of expertise can be distinguished from nonexpert objects with respect to neural activity as measured by fMRI and electrophysiological methods.

## 11 Convolutional Neural Networks: The New "Artificial" Expert

The February 2017 cover of the scientific journal *Nature* heralded the coming of a new kind of perceptual expert – the convolutional neural network (CNN). In a groundbreaking study, Esteva et al. (2017) taught a CNN to distinguish varieties of common malignant carcinomas from deadlier malignant melanomas. When tested with a novel set of lesions, the CNN performed as well or better than board-certified dermatologists in classifying both the common and serious types of melanomas. These results raise provocative questions about the similarities and differences between machine and human experts.

In this section, we begin by exploring the nuts and bolts of machine learning by examining CNNs in terms of their architecture, learning algorithms, inputs, and outputs. Next, we describe two applications of CNNs in medical diagnosis and compare the performance of AI experts to the performance of human medical experts. We then discuss the perceptual information and algorithms that CNNs employ to make their object recognition decisions and situations where these algorithms can lead to surprising and unpredictable errors. In the final section, we revisit the principles of human perceptual expertise (e.g., downward shifts in recognition, training effects, and diagnostic cues) as viewed through the lens of the CNN artificial expert.

### The Basic Architecture of Convolutional Neural Networks

In vision, the goal of the CNN is to categorize an input image at specific levels of recognition (e.g., Abraham Lincoln, Bachman's warbler, Doberman pinscher). The to-be-recognized image is presented to the CNN as a matrix of pixel values indicating its luminance and color. The pixel values in an image are not random but contain important information about the spatial contingencies embedded in the image where neighboring pixels are likely to share similar luminance values. For example, as shown in Figure 16, the outline of Lincoln's face is denoted by small luminance values that are spatially adjacent to one another. Inspired by Hubel and Wiesel's work on the mammalian visual system (Hubel & Wiesel 1962), artificial CNN is a large mathematical model with parameters that learns from the regularities in this kind of image data.

As shown in Figure 16, the input image is passed through a series of convolutional and pooling layers containing nodes of information. Units on each layer are connected by links whose connection strengths (i.e., weights) are adjusted during learning. The *convolutional layer* takes advantage of the spatial contingencies by applying filters, also known as "kernels," that are tuned to the primitive features in the image (e.g., oriented edges, colors) similar to the V1 cells in the primary visual cortex. Filters can be visualized like the light field holograms in *Star Trek* or a flashlight's spotlight that systematically scans the image from top to bottom building a feature map of diagnostic information. The activation outputs from the convolutional layer are relayed to the *pooling layer* that aggregates and reduces (i.e., downsamples) the feature maps while retaining their diagnostic properties. The layers of hidden units have local connectivity, meaning that each unit in a layer receives inputs from a small number of units in the previous layer. As shown in Figure 18b, CNNs mimic the properties of the primate visual system where the early analyses with simple oriented edge detectors are combined to form higher-order features at the later layers similarly to shape-based objects neurons found in the inferotemporal cortex (Kriegeskorte, 2015; Yamins et al., 2014). The combined outputs are projected onto the *fully connected* output layer. Recognition is a selection process by which the category node with the highest output activation is chosen among the competing candidates of objects. In supervised models, if the CNN makes a wrong recognition decision (e.g., selecting Thomas Jefferson instead of George Washington), the network receives feedback and adjusts the connection weights between the nodes in proportion to the magnitude of the error signal, using an algorithm known as "backpropagation."

For CNNs, the 2012 ImageNet Large Scale Visual Recognition Challenge was a watershed moment. The competition pitted the best neural network models against one another in a test of object recognition. The 2012 competition was the debut of AlexNet, a new kind of CNN that introduced groundbreaking advances in learning algorithms and allocation of computing resources (Krizhevsky et al., 2012). For the contest, the

(a)          DEEP LEARNING NEURAL NETWORK

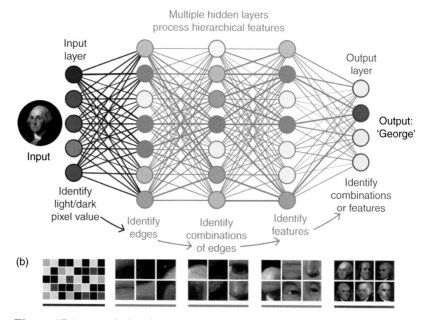

**Figure 17** A convolutional neural network (CNN): (a) a *structural* diagram of a CNN showing its basic components of an input layer, convolutional layers, pooling layers, classification units, and final output unit; (b) a *functional* diagram of a CNN showing its early layers abstracting simple oriented edges that are to form higher-order features that produce a whole object representation that is classified at the output layer (Waldrop 2019).

models were trained with the ImageNet database containing more than 5 million high-resolution images from more than 22,000 object categories. When validated with a novel set of images, AlexNet was able to recognize objects that were often centered or embedded in complex backgrounds and achieved a recognition rate of 85 percent, more than 10 percentage points higher than its nearest competitor. The success of AlexNet attracted the attention of researchers in AI and the public in general because it was one of the first demonstrations of how CNNs can be applied to solve complex problems in real-world object recognition.

## Machines versus Humans: Two Case Studies of CNNs in Medical Diagnosis

Nowhere has AI and deep learning networks made a greater impact than in the field of medical diagnosis. Here, we examine two examples in medical diagnosis, one in retinopathy and the other in breast cancer, that compare the performance of CNNs against the perceptual judgments of human experts.

Diabetic retinopathy is a complication of diabetes where high blood pressure causes damage to the eye's retina, resulting in impaired vision and in extreme cases blindness. Retinopathy is characterized by a proliferation of dark spots and neurovascular blood vessels in the retinal digital image. Conventionally, skilled ophthalmologists manually inspect retinal images of the patient and grade the photographs on a severity scale ranging from mild to severe. An important question is whether the diagnostic process can be automated through the application of CNNs. Gulshan et al. (2016) trained a CNN using a data set of 128,175 retinal images that were graded by a panel of licensed ophthalmologists and ophthalmology senior residents. Their results showed that CNNs achieved an accuracy level of 99 percent and performed as well or better than trained ophthalmologists. The CNN performed remarkably well in measures of sensitivity (the ability to correctly identify images with retinopathy) and specificity (the ability to correctly reject images that do not have retinopathy), demonstrating its diagnostic effectiveness.

Breast cancer is the most frequently diagnosed cancer among women, and the World Health Organization (WHO) estimates that the number of cancer cases expected in 2025 will be 19.3 million. One of the strongest known risk factors of breast cancer is the relative amount of radio dense tissue present in the mammogram X-ray, expressed as mammographic density (MD) where women with high MD have a two- to sixfold increased breast cancer risk compared to women with low MD (Wolfe, 1976). Fonseca et al. (2015) collected 1,157 mammogram images that were blindly classified by seven radiologists with 5 to 25 years of experience into 1 of 4 categories of breast density (1 = less dense, 4 = most dense). A CNN was trained to classify a subset of the mammogram and its performance was tested against the judgments of a subset of untrained images. The CNN demonstrated an overall accuracy rate of 73 percent and an average inter-rater reliability of 0.58, which compared favorably to individual radiologist performance inter-rater reliability that ranged from 0.56 to 0.79.

In a more recent study (Ragab et al., 2019), a CNN was trained with a database composed of more than 10,000 normal, benign, or malignant mammograms. When tested with a novel set of images, the CNN was able to classify the images as benign or cancerous at an accuracy rate of 94 percent. These examples illustrate the precision and accuracy of current

CNNs whose performance will improve over time as more efficient algorithms are developed and more extensive databases are made available.

CNN diagnoses have certain benefits over human expert decisions in that they are internally reliable as well as convenient, efficient, and noninvasive for the patient. While early detection of medical conditions through AI should significantly improve patient outcomes, it is unlikely that CNNs will completely replace human medical experts. If the everyday tasks of radiologists can be performed faster and better by AI systems, this will allow the medical expert the time to focus on solving complex clinical problems (Chiwome et al., 2020; ESR 2019). Indeed, many medical practitioners view CNNs not as replacements for diagnosticians but rather as "decision support systems" (Campanella et al., 2020).

## Different Routes to Recognition Taken by CNNs and Humans

As the foregoing examples demonstrate, CNNs perform as well or even better than skilled perceptual experts in specialized domains, such as mammography and retinopathy. Paradoxically, these same expert models commit everyday recognition errors that even a young child wouldn't make. Szegedy et al. (2014) showed that minute perturbations of an image – what are referred to as *adversarial images* – cause CNNs to misclassify images in bizarre and unpredictable ways, such as mistaking a school bus for an ostrich. Another manipulation that can cause problems for CNNs is contrast reversal causes where the negative image of a car leads to it being mislabeled as a ship (Hosseini et al., 2017). Thus, whereas the human visual system demonstrates robust object recognition across changes in the retinal input, CNNs can be vulnerable to even subtle variations in the image.

The type of recognition errors committed by CNNs reveal how their algorithms deviate from the strategies employed by humans. Geirhos et al. (2019) trained a CNN to recognize images from the ImageNet database, a library containing millions of manually annotated photographs and grouped into more than 20,000 categories. The researchers then tested the CNNs and human observers for their recognition of hybrid images that contained conflicting texture and shape cues such as a cat-shaped image with the texture of an elephant shown in Figure 18a. Whereas human observers recognize the hybrid images based on their overall shape (e.g., cat), CNNs were biased toward its texture recognition (e.g., elephant). Thus, it is possible for CNNs to identify objects based on unique combinations of local texture patches rather than integrating the patches into an object's global shape (Brendel & Bethge, 2019; Geirhos et al., 2019).

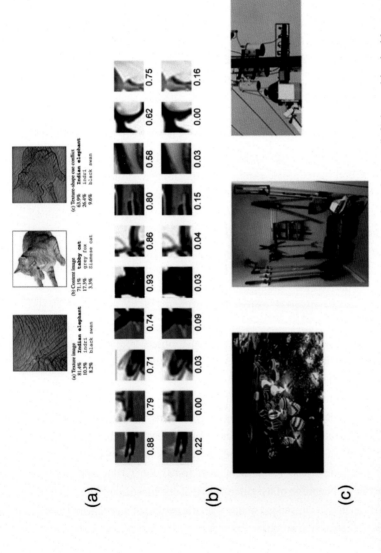

**Figure 18** Probing the object recognition strategies of CNNs: (a) the texture of an elephant (left) is combined with a cat image (middle) to form a hybrid image (right) (Geirhos et al., 2019); (b) minimal recognizable configurations (MIRCs) are small image patches that contain sufficient diagnostic information to permit object recognition – whereas human recognition performance drops drastically when the MIRC is shifted or blurred (percentage of correct human responses shown below MIRCs), in contrast the recognition performance of CNNs shows only a slight decline (Ullman et al., 2016); (c) misidentification of objects by CNNs (indicated in red box) – a hot air balloon is misidentified as a sports ball (left), a rake is misidentified as a toothbrush (middle), and telephone insulators are misidentified as an airplane (right) (Eckstein et al., 2017).

Ullman et al.(2016) explored the limits of image patches by constructing what they referred to as "minimal recognizable configurations" (MIRCs). An MIRC is a small patch of an image that contains the minimum amount of information needed to be recognizable by most human observers. Presumably, MIRCs contain enough information about the parts of an object and spatial relations to enable recognition. Critically, slight perturbations in the size, location, or resolution of the MIRC destroy these structural properties to the point where recognition is no longer possible (as shown in Figure 18b). However, these same perturbations have relatively weak effects on the recognition performance of CNNs because the altered image preserves texture information that is key to their recognition. Humans focused on specific, diagnostic part regions that remained relatively consistent across viewpoints, whereas CNN models selected features that are specific to a particular viewpoint (Karimi-Rouzbahani et al., 2017).

In our everyday experience, objects are not recognized in isolation but are part of a larger scene context. For example, when we walk into a kitchen, we expect to see certain collections of objects, such as a refrigerator, toaster, oven, or can openers, and these objects are situated at predictable locations (e.g., toaster on the counter) and are of a certain size (e.g., toasters are larger than can openers but smaller than refrigerators). For humans, scene knowledge facilitates recognition where we are faster to identify objects when they appear in the expected contexts and at expected locations (e.g., computer on an office desk) than when they are found in an unexpected scene and location (e.g., computer in a bathtub) (Biederman et al., 1982).

CNNs are less influenced by scene context and object locations than humans and tend to focus on the local properties of the object. Eckstein et al. (2017) showed that humans often miss targets that are in plain sight when they are depicted at an unusual scale (e.g., a giant toothbrush) or appear in an unexpected location (e.g., toothbrush on a rug). In contrast, CNNs had few problems finding these target objects when depicted at an unusual scale or location. At the same time, because CNNs lack scene knowledge, they commit strange recognition errors (e.g., mistaking a telephone for an airplane or misrecognizing a rake as a toothbrush) that humans would seldom make (see Figure 18c) (Eckstein et al. 2017).

Despite the putative similarities between the human and CNNs (Kriegeskorte, 2015; Kubilius et al., 2016), the foregoing studies illustrate that humans and CNNs take different routes to recognition. Whereas the human observers use prior knowledge to recognize objects and information about their parts, configuration, and external shapes, CNNs recognize objects based on their image properties (e.g., texture, surface, edges) that are linked to specific, local information contained in the training images.

## Simulating Human Perceptual Expertise in CNNs

In this section, we speculate about how CNNs can be applied to explore the computational principles behind perceptual expertise with respect to downward shifts in recognition, training and recognition biases, and the identification of diagnostic features.

*Downward Shifts in Recognition.* To facilitate their subordinate level recognition, perceptual experts are attuned to subtle variations in visual features that differentiate one subordinate level object from another (Tanaka & Taylor, 1991). A bird expert, for example, knows that a hairy woodpecker is distinguished from its close relative, the downy wood-pecker, by its elongated and larger beak. To address the challenge of fine-grain subordinate level categorizations, neural networks must have knowledge about which part or region of the object is the most diagnostic and then obtain a fine-grain feature learning from those regions that goes beyond the basic level parts (Fu et al., 2017). One solution that is time- and labor-intensive has been to recruit human annotators to identify and label the object parts in the image (Deng et al., 2013). Some methods allow the CNN to recursively identify and zoom in on discriminative regions to learn about the object part at this finer grain of detail (Fu et al., 2017). Another strategy first segments the figure object from its background to align it with objects in similar poses and then identifies the parts of the objects with similar poses to remap those regions back onto the images (Krause et al., 2015). These models demonstrate that, with additional human and machine interventions, CNNs can achieve the level of subordinate recognition exhibited by human experts.

*Experience and Training.* Like human experts, CNNs can only learn to recognize the object categories that they are exposed to during training expertise. Depending on the makeup or size of the training set, outputs can be contaminated with biased content (Gebru, 2019). For example, Camilleri et al. (2019) tested a CNN and acutely demonstrated it had racial, gender, and age bias in its predictions because the training images gathered were primarily of celebrities, a category that is disproportion-ately white, male, and more youthful looking than the general population. Even with retraining they were only able to make incremental improve-ments to correct this tendency once learned (Camilleri et al., 2019).

Critical studies have shown that some CNNs are more likely to classify criminal defendants who are black as more likely to reoffend than those who are white (Angwin et al., 2016) and that many natural language processing tools, having been trained using newspapers, exhibit societal biases in their outputs, such as finishing the analogy "man is to computer programmer as woman is to [x]" with "homemaker" (Gebru, 2019). Just like human experts, these cases show that CNNs make judgments on the basis of their initial training experiences. Therefore, biases in the training set will be reflected in biases in the output recognition with limited transfer within the category domain to another (Tanaka et al., 2005).

*Diagnostic Features.* In the expertise research, much attention has been devoted to identifying the diagnostic object properties that facilitate subordinate level recognition, such as an object's parts (Johnson & Mervis, 1997; Tanaka & Taylor, 1991), its color (Devillez et al., 2019; Hagen et al., 2014; Jones et al., 2018), and SF information (Hagen et al., 2016; Harel & Bentin, 2009; Jones et al., 2018). While many CNNs excel at recognition, they are "black boxes" where the basis for their decisions is not accessible. For example, though we know that the CNN accurately identifies a cat in a picture, we can't understand the exact mechanism or chain of reasoning by which it generates this result. A picture of a cat showing its incisors might require less convolutions to identify than a picture of a cat with a party hat on its head. Interestingly, though the semantic label "cat" could be outputted for ten pictures of cats, the exact reasoning process of the CNNs could be theoretically unique for each. Though we know an algorithm employs *some* process of reasoning, the nature of its logic, or even whether its logic is consistent across calculations, cannot be secured through an analysis of its finished product alone. Explainable AI (XAI) methods are being actively developed to provide justifications for results in order to prevent unwarranted causal explanations and to secure human trust in AI outputs (Rieger et al., 2020). The machine learning community is also starting to explore new architectures that rival or exceed CNNs, such as the Visual Transformer, but they need to be trained with larger data sets to reveal these benefits (Dosovitskiy et al., 2020). It is an open question whether these approaches will better model human visual perception compared to the conventional CNN architecture.

In this section, we discussed CNNs as the new perceptual expert whose recognition performance rivals and even exceeds the performance of seasoned human experts. However, the route to expert recognition for

CNNs seems to be different than the strategies employed by human perceptual experts. Unlike human experts, CNNs do not seem to abstract representation of parts but recognize objects based on their distinctive image patches (Geirhos et al., 2019). Although the patch approach serves CNNs well in specialized domains, such as melanoma diagnosis (Esteva et al., 2017) and retinopathy (Gulshan et al., 2016), this approach can lead to unpredictable errors in everyday object recognition (Waldrop, 2019). Despite their shortcomings, CNNs hold promise for elucidating the computational principles of perceptual expertise involved in subordinate level recognition, the role of learning experience, and identification of diagnostic recognition cues.

## 12 Wrapping Up and Concluding Thoughts

This Element asked how experience changes the way we see the world. To answer, we presented the effects of extensive domain-specific experience on object recognition in perceptual experts like birdwatchers, dog judges, and car aficionados. We proposed the downward shift hypothesis as a means of predicting how experts differ from novices; whereas novices first recognize and identify objects at the basic level of categorization, we hypothesized that experts recognize the same object at the subordinate level (Rosch et al., 1976). Confirmation of the downward shift hypothesis was exhibited in studies of real-world experts (Johnson & Mervis, 1997; Tanaka & Taylor, 1991) and laboratory-trained participants (Gauthier & Tarr 1997; Jones et al., 2018; Scott et al., 2006, 2008). By recognizing objects in their domain of expertise at a lower level of the conceptual hierarchy, experts truly see the world from a different perspective than novices.

Perceptual expertise varies. In its most narrow form, people can demonstrate perceptual expertise for a single object of personal ownership such as an item of clothing (Miyakoshi et al., 2007) or for a familiar landmark (Anaki & Bentin, 2009). In contrast, societal groups of many members can display a homogeneous downward shift in recognition for those objects that are particularly meaningful and relevant in their everyday lives. For instance, members of the Tzeltal culture in Mexico routinely identify plants by their subordinate folk genera names (e.g., aspen, oak, redwood, and monkey tree) rather than the basic level term "tree" preferred by people from industrial societies. Perceptual experts can be found at all ages as exhibited by children with EII and children on the autism spectrum whose obsessions with objects, such as dinosaurs (Gobbo & Chi, 1986), shore birds (Johnson & Mervis, 1997), and Pokémon characters (Grelotti et al. 2005; Gomez et al. 2019), produce the same kind of downward shift in recognition observed in adult experts.

At the perceptual level, experts are tuned to visual details such as the color of objects in their domain of expertise (Devillez et al., 2019; Hagen et al., 2014, 2016; Harel & Bentin, 2009). One compelling view to explain expertise is the idea that experts form holistic representations of subordinate level objects so that these objects shift from being perceived in terms of their parts to being perceived as wholes. These template-like representations can be disrupted by inversion (Campbell & Tanaka, 2018; Diamond & Carey, 1986). Expertise is manifested in the cognitive behaviors of the expert and is exhibited by experts locating expert objects faster (Hershler & Hochstein, 2009; McGugin et al., 2011), encoding expert objects quicker (Curby & Gauthier, 2009), and finding expert objects more memorable than nonexpert objects (Curby et al., 2009; Curby & Gauthier, 2010).

The behavioral changes brought on by perceptual expertise are accompanied by changes in brain function. Neuroimaging findings show that real-world experts (Gauthier et al., 2000), laboratory-trained experts (Gauthier et al., 1999), and young children with special interests (Grelotti et al., 2005; Gomez et al., 2019; James & James, 2013) show enhanced activation of the FFA when viewing objects of expertise (Kanwisher et al., 1997; Kanwisher & Yovel, 2006). Studies employing electrophysiological methods have shown that the N170 and N250 brain components that are commonly associated with face processing are activated during expert recognition. Thus, the brain structures and neural dynamics that are associated with face expertise are engaged when perceptual experts see other types of objects in their domain of expertise.

In recent years, CNNs have emerged as a new kind of perceptual expert. When matched against human experts, CNNs do as well or even surpass the judgments of experienced professionals (Esteva et al., 2017; Gulshan et al., 2016). However, the paths to recognition for CNNs seem different than the routes taken by humans. CNN classifications analyze small image patches of the image in contrast to the part structure and global information used by the human expert (Geirhos et al., 2019). Occasionally, images containing minute pixel changes (i.e., adversarial images) that are imperceptible to the human eye can produce unpredictable errors and bizarre misrecognitions in CNNs (Szegedy et al., 2014). Despite these human and machine differences, CNNs are promising tools for probing computational aspects of perceptual expertise involving subordinate level recognition (Fu et al., 2017; Ullman et al., 2016; Deng et al., 2013), training biases (Buolamwini & Gebru, 2018), and identifying the diagnostic cues of expertise (Rieger et al., 2020).

In conclusion, the collective evidence on perceptual expertise demonstrates that experience shapes how we recognize objects in the world. Based on extensive experience and training, experts recognize objects from their domain of expertise at a more specific, subordinate level than novices. Hence, contrary to Eleanor Rosch's "structure in the world" view, there is no universal, basic level of object recognition. Instead, what determines the level at which we first recognize an object is in the *eye, mind, and experience of the beholder.*

# References

Aldridge, R. B., Maxwell, S. S., & Rees, J. L. (2012). Dermatology undergraduate skin cancer training: A disconnect between recommendations, clinical exposure and competence. *BMC Medical Education*, *12*(1), 1–9. https://doi.org/10.1186/1472-6920-12-27

Alexander, J. M., Johnson, K. E., Leibham, M. E., & Kelley, K. (2008). The development of conceptual interests in young children. *Cognitive Development*, *23*(2), 324–334. https://doi.org/10.1016/j.cogdev.2007.11.004

Alvarez, G. A. & Cavanagh, P. (2004). The capacity of visual short-term memory is set both by visual information load and by number of objects. *Psychological Science*, *15*(2), 106–111. https://doi.org/10.1111/j.0963-7214.2004.01502006.x

Anaki, D. & Bentin, S. (2009). Familiarity effects on categorization levels of faces and objects. *Cognition*, *111*(1), 144–149.

Anglin, J. M. (1977). *Word, Object, and Conceptual Development*. New York: W. W. Norton.

Angwin, J., Larson, J., Mattu, S., and Kirchner, L. (2016). Machine bias: There's software across the country to predict future criminals and it's biased against blacks. *ProPublica*.

Ashby, F. G. & Ell, S. W. (2001). The neurobiology of human category learning. *Trends in Cognitive Sciences*, *5*(5), 204–210. www.ncbi.nlm.nih.gov/pubmed/11323265

Ashby, G. F. & O'Brien, J. B. (2005). Category learning and multiple memory systems. *Trends in Cognitive Sciences*, *9*(2), 83–89. https://doi.org/10.1016/j.tics.2004.12.003

Baron-Cohen, S., Ashwin, E., Ashwin, C., Tavassoli, T., & Chakrabarti, B. (2009). Talent in autism: Hyper-systemizing, hyper-attention to detail and sensory hypersensitivity. *Philosophical Transactions of the Royal Society B: Biological Sciences*, *364*(1522), 1377–1383. https://doi.org/10.1098/rstb.2008.0337

Baron-Cohen, S. & Wheelwright, S. (1999). "Obsessions" in children with autism or Asperger syndrome: Content analysis in terms of core domains of cognition. *British Journal of Psychiatry*, *175*(5), 484–490.

Barragan-Jason, G., Lachat, F., & Barbeau, E. (2012). How fast is famous face recognition? *Frontiers in Psychology*, *3*, 454.

Barton, J. J. S., Hantif, H., & Ashraf, S. (2009). Relating visual to verbal semantic knowledge: The evaluation of object recognition in prosopagnosia. *Brain*, *132*(12), 3456–3466. https://doi.org/10.1093/brain/awp252

Belke, B., Leder, H., Harsanyi, G., & Carbon, C. C. (2010). When a Picasso is a "Picasso": The entry point in the identification of visual art. *Acta Psychologica*, *133*(2), 191–202. https://doi.org/10.1016/j.actpsy.2009.11.007

Biederman, I. & Ju, G. (1988). Surface versus edge-based determinants of visual recognition. *Cognitive Psychology*, *20*(1), 38–64.

Biederman, I., Mezzanotte, R. J., & Rabinowitz, J. C. (1982). Scene perception: Detecting and judging objects undergoing relational violations. *Cognitive Psychology*, *14*(2), 143–177.

Biederman, I. & Shiffrar, M. (1987). Sexing day-old chicks: A case-study and expert systems-analysis of a difficult perceptual-learning task. *Journal of Experimental Psychology: Learning Memory and Cognition*, *13*(4), 640–645.

Bilalić, M., Grottenthaler, T., Nagele, T., & Lindig, T. (2016). The faces in radiological images: Fusiform face area supports radiological expertise. *Cerebral Cortex*, *26*(3), 1004–1014. https://doi.org/10.1093/cercor/bhu272

Bilalić, M., Langner, R., Ulrich, R., & Grodd, W. (2011). Many faces of expertise: Fusiform face area in chess experts and novices. *Journal of Neuroscience*, *31*(28), 10206–10214. https://doi.org/10.1523/JNEUROSCI.5727-10.2011

Bornstein, M. H. & Arterberry, M. E. (2010). The development of object categorization in young children: Hierarchical inclusiveness, age, perceptual attribute, and group versus individual analyses. *Developmental Psychology*, *46*(2), 350–365. https://doi.org/10.1037/a0018411

Boster, J. S. & Johnson, J. C. (1989). Form or function: A comparison of expert and novice judgments of similarity among fish. *American Anthropologist*, *91*(4), 866–889.

Braje, W. L., Tjan, B. S., & Legge, G. E. (1995). Human efficiency for recognizing and detecting low-pass filtered objects. *Vision Research*, *35*(21), 2955–2966. https://doi.org/10.1016/0042-6989(95)00071-7

Bramão, I., Inacio, F., Faísca, L., Reis, A., & Petersson, K. M. (2011). The influence of color information on the recognition of color diagnostic and noncolor diagnostic objects. *Journal of General Psychology*, *138*(1), 49–65. https://doi.org/10.1080/00221309.2010.533718

Brendel, W. & Bethge, M. (2019). Approximating CNNs with bag-of-local-features models works surprisingly well on ImageNet. arXiv:1904.00760, 1–15.

Brown, R. (1958). How shall a thing be called? *Psychological Review*, *65*(1), 14–21. https://doi.org/10.1037/h0041727

Bruyer, R. & Crispeels, G. (1992). Expertise in person recognition. *Bulletin of the Psychonomic Society*, *30*(6), 501–504. https://doi.org/10.3758/BF03334112

Bukach, C. M., Vickery, T. J., Kinka, D., & Gauthier, I. (2012). Training experts: Individuation without naming is worth it. *Journal of Experimental Psychology: Human Perception and Performance*, *38*(1), 14–17.

Buolamwini, J. & Gebru, T. (2018). Gender shades: Intersectional accuracy disparities in commercial gender classification. In *Conference on Fairness, Accountability and Transparency*, 77–91. *PMLR*.

Busey, T. A. & Vanderkolk, J. R. (2005). Behavioral and electrophysiological evidence for configural processing in fingerprint experts. *Vision Research*, *45*(4), 431–448. https://doi.org/10.1016/j.visres.2004.08.021

Callanan, M. A. (1985). How parents label objects for young children: The role of input in the acquisition of category hierarchies. *Child Development*, 508–523. https://doi.org/10.2307/1129738

Camilleri, A., Geoghegan, R., Meade, R., Osorio, S., & Zou., Q. (2019). Bias in machine learning: How facial recognition models show signs of racism, sexism and ageism. *Towards Data Science*, December 14. https://towardsdatascience.com/bias-in-machine-learning-how-facial-recognition-models-show-signs-of-racism-sexism-and-ageism-32549e2c972d (accessed February 18, 2021)

Campanella, G., Nehal, K. S., Lee, E. H., Rossi, A., Possum, B., Manuel, G., ... & Busam, K. J. (2021). A deep learning algorithm with high sensitivity for the detection of basal cell carcinoma in Mohs micrographic surgery frozen sections. *Journal of the American Academy of Dermatology*, 85(5), 1285–1286.

Campbell, A. & Tanaka, J. W. (2018). Inversion impairs expert budgerigar identity recognition: A face-like effect for a nonface object of expertise. *Perception*, *47*(6), 647–659. https://doi.org/10.1177/0301006618771806

Carrigan, A. J., Wardle, S. G., & Rich, A. N. (2018). Finding cancer in mammograms: If you know it's there, do you know where? *Cognitive Research: Principles and Implications*, 3(1), 1–14.

Chen, S. C., Bravata, D. M., Weil, E., & Olkin, I. (2001). A comparison of dermatologists' and primary care physicians' accuracy in diagnosing melanoma: A systematic review. *Archives of Dermatology*, 137(12), 1627–1634.

Chin, M. D., Evans, K. K., Wolfe, J. M., Bowen, J., & Tanaka, J. W. (2018). Inversion effects in the expert classification of mammograms and faces. *Cognitive Research: Principles and Implications*, 3(1), 1–9, *17*(10). https://doi.org/10.1167/17.10.1226

Chiwome, L., Okojie, O. M., Jamiur, A. K., Javed, F., & Hamid, P. (2020). Artificial intelligence: Is it Armageddon for breast radiologists? *Cureus*, *12*(6). https://doi.org/10.7759/cureus.8923

Collin, C. A. & McMullen, P. A. (2005). Subordinate-level categorization relies on high spatial frequencies to a greater degree than basic-level categorization. *Perception and Psychophysics*, *67*(2), 354–364. www.ncbi.nlm.nih.gov/pubmed/15971697

Costen, N. P., Parker, D. M., & Craw, I. (1994). Spatial content and spatial quantisation effects in face recognition. *Perception*, *23*(2), 129–146. https://doi.org/10.1068/p230129

Costen, N. P., Parker, D. M., & Craw, I. (1996). Effects of high-pass and low-pass spatial filtering on face identification. *Perception and Psychophysics*, *58*(4), 602–612. https://doi.org/10.3758/BF03213093

Curby, K. M. & Gauthier, I. (2009). The temporal advantage for individuating objects of expertise: Perceptual expertise is an early riser. *Journal of Vision*, 9(6), 1–13. https://doi.org/10.1167/9.6.7.

Curby, K. M., Glazek, K., & Gauthier, I. (2009). A visual short-term memory advantage for objects of expertise. *Journal of Experimental Psychology: Human Perception and Performance*, *35*(1), 94–107.

Curby, K. M. & Gauthier, I. (2010). To the trained eye: Perceptual expertise alters visual processing. *Topics in Cognitive Science*, *2*(2), 189–201.

Curran, T., Tanaka, J. W., & Weiskopf, D. M. (2002). An electrophysiological comparison of visual categorization and recognition memory. *Cognitive Affective and Behavioral Neuroscience*, *2*(1), 1–18. https://doi.org/10.3758/CABN.2.1.1

Davidoff, J. & Donnelly, N. (1990). Object superiority: A comparison of complete and part probes. *Acta Psychologica*, *73*(3), 225–243.

DeLoache, J. S., Simcock, G., & Macari, S. (2007). Planes, trains, automobiles – and tea sets: Extremely intense interests in very young children. *Developmental Psychology*, *43*(6), 1579–1586. https://doi.org/10.1037/0012-1649.43.6.1579

Deng, J., Krause, J., & Fei-Fei, L. (2013). Fine-grained crowdsourcing for fine-grained recognition. *Proceedings of the IEEE Conference on Computer Vision and Pattern Recognition*, 580–587.

Dennett, H. W., McKone, E., Tavashmi, R. et al. (2012). The Cambridge Car Memory Test: A task matched in format to the Cambridge Face Memory Test, with norms, reliability, sex differences, dissociations from face memory, and expertise effects. *Behavior Research Methods*, *44*(2), 587–605. https://doi .org/10.3758/s13428-011-0160-2

Devillez, H., Mollison, M. V., Hagen, S., Tanaka, J. W., Scott, L. S., & Curran, T. (2019). Color and spatial frequency differentially impact early stages of perceptual expertise training. *Neuropsychologia*, *122*, 62–75. https://doi.org/10.1016/j.neuropsychologia.2018.11.011

Diamond, R. & Carey, S. (1986). Why faces are not special: An effect of expertise. *Journal of Experimental Psychology: General*, *115*(2), 107–117.

Dosovitskiy, A., Beyer, L., Kolesnikov, A. et al. (2020). An image is worth 16×16 words: Transformers for image recognition at scale. arXiv. http://arxiv.org/abs/2010.11929

Dougherty, J. W. D. (1978). Salience and relativity in classification. *American Ethnologist*, *5*(1), 66–80. https://doi.org/10.1525/ae.1978.5.1.02a00060

Eckstein, M. P., Koehler, K., Welbourne, L. E., & Akbas, E. (2017). Humans, but not deep neural networks, often miss giant targets in scenes. *Current Biology: CB*, *27*(18), 2827–2832.e3.

ESR (European Society of Radiology). (2019). What the radiologist should know about artificial intelligence: An ESR white paper. *Insights Imaging*, *10* (1), 44. https://doi.org/10.1186/s13244-019-0738-2

Esteva, A., Kuprel, B., Novoa, R. A. et al. (2017). Dermatologist-level classification of skin cancer with deep neural networks. *Nature*, *542*(7639), 115–118.

Evans, K. K., Georgian-Smith, D., Tambouret, R., Birdwell, R. L., & Wolfe, J. M. (2013). The gist of the abnormal: Above-chance medical decision making in the blink of an eye. *Psychonomic Bulletin and Review*, *20*(6), 1170–1175. https://doi.org/10.3758/s13423-013-0459-3.

Evans, K. K., Haygood, T. M., Cooper, J., Culpan, A.-M., & Wolfe, J. M. (2016). A half-second glimpse often lets radiologists identify breast cancer cases even when viewing the mammogram of the opposite breast. *Proceedings of the National Academy of Sciences of the United States of America*, *113*(37), 10292–10297.

Fan, C., He, W., He, H., Ren, G., Luo, Y., Li, H., & Luo, W. (2016). N170 changes show identifiable Chinese characters compete primarily with faces rather than houses. *Frontiers in Psychology*, *6*, 1952. https://doi.org/10.3389/ fpsyg.2015.01952

Fonseca, P., Mendoza, J., Wainer, J. et al. (2015). Automatic breast density classification using a convolutional neural network architecture search procedure. *Medical Imaging 2015: Computer-Aided Diagnosis, 9414,* 941428.

Foss-Feig, J. H., McGugin, R. W., Gauthier, I., Mash, L. E., Ventola, P., & Cascio, C. J. (2016). A functional neuroimaging study of fusiform response to restricted interests in children and adolescents with autism spectrum disorder. *Journal of Neurodevelopmental Disorders, 8*(1), 1–12. https://doi .org/10.1186/s11689-016-9149-6

Fu, J., Zheng, H., & Mei, T. (2017). Look closer to see better: Recurrent attention convolutional neural network for fine-grained image recognition. *Proceedings of the IEEE Conference on Computer Vision and Pattern Recognition,* 4438–4446.

Gauthier, I., Curran, T., Curby, K. M., & Collins, D. (2003). Perceptual interference supports a non-modular account of face processing. *Nature Neuroscience, 6*(4), 428–432. https://doi.org/10.1038/nn1029nn

Gauthier, I., Skudlarski, P., Gore, J. C., & Anderson, A. W. (2000). Expertise for cars and birds recruits brain areas involved in face recognition. *Nature Neuroscience, 3,* 191–197.

Gauthier, I. & Tarr, M. J. (1997). Becoming a "Greeble" expert: Exploring the face recognition mechanism. *Vision Research, 37*(12), 1673–1682.

Gauthier, I., Tarr, M. J., Anderson, A. W., Skudlarski, P., & Gore, J. C. (1999). Activation of the middle fusiform "face area" increases with expertise in recognizing novel objects. *Nature Neuroscience, 2*(6), 568–573.

Gauthier, I., Williams, P., Tarr, M. J., & Tanaka, J. (1998). Training "greeble" experts: A framework for studying expert object recognition processes. *Vision Research, 38*(15–16). https://doi.org/10.1016/S0042-6989(97) 00442-2

Gebru, T. (2019). Oxford handbook on AI ethics book chapter on race and gender. arXiv preprint arXiv:1908.06165.

Gegenfurtner, K. R. & Rieger, J. (2000). Sensory and cognitive contributions of color to the recognition of natural scenes. *Current Biology: CB, 10*(13), 805–808. www.ncbi.nlm.nih.gov/pubmed/10898985

Geirhos, R., Michaelis, C., Wichmann, F. A., Rubisch, P., Bethge, M., & Brendel, W. (2019). Imagenet-trained CNNs are biased towards texture; increasing shape bias improves accuracy and robustness. *7th International Conference on Learning Representations, ICLR 2019, c,* 1–22.

Glover, G. H. (2011). Overview of functional magnetic resonance imaging. *Neurosurgery Clinics of North America, 22*(2), 133–139. https://doi.org/ 10.1016/j.nec.2010.11.001

Gobbo, C. & Chi, M. (1986). How knowledge is structured and used by expert and novice children. *Cognitive Development, 1*(3), 221–237.

Goffaux, V., Hault, B., Michel, C., Vuong, Q. C., & Rossion, B. (2005). The respective role of low and high spatial frequencies in supporting configural and featural processing of faces. *Perception, 34*(1), 77–86. https://doi.org/10.1068/p5370

Gomez, J., Barnett, M., & Grill-Spector, K. (2019). Extensive childhood experience with Pokémon suggests eccentricity drives organization of visual cortex. *Nature Human Behaviour 3*(6), 611–624. https://doi.org/10.1038/s41562-019-0592-8

Grelotti, D. J., Klin, A. J., Gauthier, I. et al. (2005). fMRI activation of the fusiform gyrus and amygdala to cartoon characters but not to faces in a boy with autism. *Neuropsychologia, 43*(3), 373–385. https://doi.org/10.1016/j.neuropsychologia.2004.06.015

Gulshan, V., Peng, L., Coram, M. et al. (2016). Development and validation of a deep learning algorithm for detection of diabetic retinopathy in retinal fundus photographs. *JAMA: The Journal of the American Medical Association, 316*(22), 2402–2410.

Hagen, S. & Tanaka, J. W. (2019). Examining the neural correlates of within-category discrimination in face and non-face expert recognition. *Neuropsychologia, 124*, 44–54.

Hagen, S., Vuong, Q. C., Scott, L. S., Curran, T., & Tanaka, J. W. (2014). The role of color in expert object recognition. *Journal of Vision, 14*(9). https://doi.org/10.1167/14.9.9

Hagen, S., Vuong, Q. C., Scott, L. S., Curran, T., & Tanaka, J. W. (2016). The role of spatial frequency in expert object recognition. *Journal of Experimental Psychology: Human Perception and Performance, 42*(3). https://doi.org/10.1037/xhp0000139

Hajibayova, L. & Jacob, E. (2015). Basic-level concepts and the assessment of subject relevance: Are they really relevant? *NASKO, 5*(1), 74–81.

Harel, A. & Bentin, S. (2009). Stimulus type, level of categorization, and spatial-frequencies utilization: Implications for perceptual categorization hierarchies. *Journal of Experimental Psychology: Human Perception and Performance, 35*(4), 1264–1273. https://doi.org/10.1037/a0013621

Harel, A., Gilaie-Dotan, S., Malach, R., & Bentin, S. (2010). Top-down engagement modulates the neural expressions of visual expertise. *Cerebral Cortex, 20*(10), 2304–2318. https://doi.org/10.1093/cercor/bhp316

Harley, E. M., Pope, W. B., Villablanca, J. P. et al. (2009). Engagement of fusiform cortex and disengagement of lateral occipital cortex in the acquisition of radiological expertise. *Cerebral Cortex, 19*(11), 2746–2754. https://doi.org/10.1093/cercor/bhp051

Hershler, O. & Hochstein, S. (2009). The importance of being expert: Top-down attentional control in visual search with photographs. *Attention, Perception, and Psychophysics*, *71*(7), 1439–1459. https://doi.org/10.3758/APP

Hosseini, H., Xiao, B., Jaiswal, M., & Poovendran, R. (2017). On the limitation of convolutional neural networks in recognizing negative images. *2017 16th IEEE International Conference on Machine Learning and Applications (ICMLA)*, 352–358.

Hsiao, J. H. & Cottrell, G. W. (2009). Not all visual expertise is holistic, but it may be leftist: The case of Chinese character recognition: Research Article. *Psychological Science*, *20*(4), 455–463. https://doi.org/10.1111/j.1467-9280.2009.02315.x

Huang, W., Wu, X., Hu, L., Wang, L., Ding, Y., & Qu, Z. (2017). Revisiting the earliest electrophysiological correlate of familiar face recognition. *International Journal of Psychophysiology*, *120*(May), 42–53. https://doi.org/10.1016/j.ijpsycho.2017.07.001

Hubel, D. H. & Wiesel, T. N. (1962). Receptive fields, binocular interaction and functional architecture in the cat's visual cortex. *The Journal of Physiology*, *160*, 106–154.

James, T. W. & James, K. H. (2013). Expert individuation of objects increases activation in the fusiform face area of children. *NeuroImage*, *67*, 182–192. https://doi.org/10.1016/j.neuroimage.2012.11.007

Johnson, K. E. & Eilers, A. T. (1998). Effects of knowledge and development on subordinate level categorization. *Cognitive Development*, *13*(4), 515–545. https://doi.org/10.1016/S0885-2014(98)90005-3

Johnson, K. E. & Mervis, C. B. (1994). Microgenetic analysis of first steps in children's acquisition of expertise on shorebirds. *Developmental Psychology*, *30*(3), 418–435. https://doi.org/10.1037/0012-1649.30.3.418

Johnson, K. E. & Mervis, C. B. (1997). Effects of varying levels of expertise on the basic level of categorization. *Journal of Experimental Psychology: General*, *126*(3), 248–277. www.ncbi.nlm.nih.gov/pubmed/9281832

Johnson, K. E., Scott, P., & Mervis, C. B. (2004). What are theories for? Concept use throughout the continuum of dinosaur expertise. *Journal of Experimental Child Psychology*, *87*(3), 171–200. https://doi.org/10.1016/j.jecp.2003.12.001

Jolicoeur, P., Gluck, M. A., & Kosslyn, S. M. (1984). Pictures and names: Making the connection. *Cognitive Psychology*, *16*(2), 243–275.

Jones, T., Hadley, H., Cataldo, A. M. et al. (2018). Neural and behavioral effects of subordinate-level training of novel objects across manipulations of color and spatial frequency. *European Journal of Neuroscience*, *52*(11), 4468–4479. https://doi.org/10.1111/ejn.13889

Kanwisher, N. (2000). Domain specificity in face perception. *Nature Neuroscience*, *3*(8), 759–763.

Kanwisher, N., McDermott, J., & Chun, M. M. (1997). The fusiform face area: A module in human extrastriate cortex specialized for face perception. *Journal of Neuroscience*, *17*(11), 4302–4311. https://doi.org/10.1523/JNEUROSCI.17-11-04302.1997

Kanwisher, N. & Yovel, G. (2006). The fusiform face area: A cortical region specialized for the perception of faces. *Philosophical transactions of the Royal Society of London: Series B, Biological Sciences*, *361*(1476), 2109–2128. https://doi.org/10.1098/rstb.2006.1934

Karimi-Rouzbahani, H., Bagheri, N., & Ebrahimpour, R. (2017). Invariant object recognition is a personalized selection of invariant features in humans, not simply explained by hierarchical feedforward vision models. *Scientific Reports*, *7*(1), 14402. https://doi.org/10.1038/s41598-017-13756-8

Klin, A., Danovitch, J. H., Merz, A. B., & Volkmar, F. R. (2007). Circumscribed interests in higher functioning individuals with autism spectrum disorders: An exploratory study. *Research and Practice for Persons with Severe Disabilities*, *32*(2), 89–100. https://doi.org/10.2511/rpsd.32.2.89

Krause, J., Jin, H., Yang, J., & Fei-Fei, L. (2015). Fine-grained recognition without part annotations. *Proceedings of the IEEE Conference on Computer Vision and Pattern Recognition*, 5546–5555.

Kriegeskorte, N. (2015). Deep neural networks: A new framework for modeling biological vision and brain information processing. *Annual Review of Vision Science*, *1*, 417–446.

Krizhevsky, A., Sutskever, I., & Hinton, G. E. (2012). Imagenet classification with deep convolutional neural networks. *Advances in Neural Information Processing Systems*, *25*, 1097–1105.

Kubilius, J., Bracci, S., & Op de Beeck, H. P. (2016). Deep neural networks as a computational model for human shape sensitivity. *PLoS Computational Biology*, *12*(4), e1004896.

Kundel, H. L. & Nodine, C. F. (1975). Interpreting chest radiographs without visual search. *Radiology*, *116*(3), 527–532. https://doi.org/10.1148/116.3.527

Krupinski, E. A. & Jiang, Y. (2008). Anniversary paper: Evaluations of medical imaging systems. *Medical Physics*, *35*(2), 645–659. https://doi.org/10.1118/1.2830376

Lebrecht, S., Pierce, L. J., Tarr, M. J., & Tanaka, J. W. (2009). Perceptual other-race training reduces implicit racial bias. *PloS One*, *4*(1), e4215.

Liu-Shuang, J., Norcia, A. M., & Rossion, B. (2014). An objective index of individual face discrimination in the right occipito-temporal cortex by means of fast periodic oddball stimulation. *Neuropsychologia, 52,* 57–72.

Luck, Steven J. (2014). *An introduction to the event-related potential technique.* Cambridge, MA: MIT Press.

Malt, B. C. (1995). Category coherence in cross-cultural perspective. *Cognitive Psychology, 29*(2), 85–148.

Margalit, E., Jamison, K. W., Weiner, K. S. et al. (2020). Ultra-high-resolution fMRI of human ventral temporal cortex reveals differential representation of categories and domains. *Journal of Neuroscience, 40*(15), 3008–3024. https://doi.org/10.1523/JNEUROSCI.2106-19.2020

Martinez-Cuitino, M. & Vivas, L. (2019). Category or diagnosticity effect? The influence of color in picture naming tasks. *Psychology and Neuroscience, 12* (3), 328–341. https://doi.org/10.1037/pne0000172

Maurer, U., Zevin, J. D., & McCandliss, B. D. (2008). Left-lateralized N170 effects of visual expertise in reading: Evidence from Japanese syllabic and logographic scripts. *Journal of Cognitive Neuroscience, 20*(10), 1878–1891. https://doi.org/10.1162/jocn.2008.20125

McGugin, R. W., Gatenby, J. C., Gore, J. C., & Gauthier, I. (2012). High-resolution imaging of expertise reveals reliable object selectivity in the fusiform face area related to perceptual performance. *Proceedings of the National Academy of Sciences of the United States of America, 109*(42), 17063–17068. https://doi.org/10.1073/pnas.1116333109

McGugin, R. W., McKeeff, T. J., Tong, F., & Gauthier, I. (2011). Irrelevant objects of expertise compete with faces during visual search. *Attention, Perception, and Psychophysics, 73*(2), 309–317. https://doi.org/10.3758/s13414-010-0006-5

Medin, D. L., Lynch, E. B., Coley, J. D., & Atran, S. (1997). Categorization and reasoning among tree experts: Do all roads lead to Rome? *Cognitive Psychology, 32*(1), 49–96. https://doi.org/10.1006/cogp.1997.0645

Miyakoshi, M., Nomura, M., & Ohira, H. (2007). An ERP study on self-relevant object recognition. *Brain and Cognition, 63*(2), 182–189.

Morrison, D. J. & Schyns, P. G. (2001). Usage of spatial scales for the categorization of faces, objects, and scenes. *Psychonomic Bulletin and Review, 8*(3), 454–469. www.ncbi.nlm.nih.gov/pubmed/11700896

Murphy, G. L. (2016). Explaining the basic-level concept advantage in infants ... or is it the superordinate-level advantage? *Psychology of Learning and Motivation: Advances in Research and Theory, 64,* 57–92.

Murphy, G. L. & Brownell, H. H. (1985). Category differentiation in object recognition: Typicality constraints on the basic category advantage. *Journal of Experimental Psychology: Learning, Memory, and Cognition*, *11*(1), 70–84.

Murphy, G. L. & Smith, E. E. (1982). Basic level superiority in picture categorization. *Journal of Verbal Learning and Verbal Behavior*, *21*(1), 1–20.

Nagai, J. & Yokosawa, K. (2003). What regulates the surface color effect in object recognition: Color diagnosticity or category. *Technical Report on Attention and Cognition*, *28*(28), 1–4. http://staff.aist.go.jp/jun.kawahara/AandC/3/nagai.pdf

Oliveria, S. A., Nehal, K. S., Christos, P. J., Sharma, N., Tromberg, J. S., & Halpern, A. C. (2001). Using nurse practitioners for skin cancer screening: A pilot study. *American Journal of Preventive Medicine*, *21*(3), 214–217.

Peterson, R. T. (1998). *Peterson First Guide to Birds of North America*. New York: Houghton Mifflin Harcourt.

Pierce, L. J., Scott, L., Boddington, S., Droucker, D., Curran, T., & Tanaka, J. (2011). The n250 brain potential to personally familiar and newly learned faces and objects. *Frontiers in Human Neuroscience*, *5*, 111.Ragab, D. A., Sharkas, M., Marshall, S., & Ren, J. (2019). Breast cancer detection using deep convolutional neural networks and support vector machines. *PeerJ*, 7, e6201. https://doi.org/10.7717/peerj.6201

Rama Fiorini, S., Gärdenfors, P., & Abel, M. (2014). Representing part-whole relations in conceptual spaces. *Cognitive Processing*, *15*(2), 127–142. https://doi.org/10.1007/s10339-013-0585-x

Richler, J. J., Wilmer, J. B., & Gauthier, I. (2017). General object recognition is specific: Evidence from novel and familiar objects. *Cognition*, *166*, 42–55.

Rieger, L., Singh, C., Murdoch, W., & Yu, B. (2020). Interpretations are useful: Penalizing explanations to align neural networks with prior knowledge. In H. D. Iii & A. Singh (Eds.), *Proceedings of the 37th International Conference on Machine Learning 119, 8116–8126. PMLR.*

Roads, B. D., Xu, B., Robinson, J. K., & Tanaka, J. W. (2018). The easy-to-hard training advantage with real-world medical images. *Cognitive Research*, *3*(38). http://doi.org/10.1186/s41235-018-0131-6

Robbins, R. & McKone, E. (2007). No face-like processing for objects-of-expertise in three behavioural tasks. *Cognition*, *103*(1), 34–79. https://doi.org/10.1016/j.cognition.2006.02.008

Rosch, E., Mervis, C. B., Gray, W., Johnson, D., & Boyes-Braem, P. (1976). Basic objects in natural categories. *Cognitive Psychology*, *8*, 382–439.

Rossion, B. (2008). Constraining the cortical face network by neuroimaging studies of acquired prosopagnosia. *NeuroImage, 40*, 423–426.

Rossion, B. (2013). The composite face illusion: A whole window into our understanding of holistic face perception. *Visual Cognition, 21*(2), 139–253. https://doi.org/10.1080/13506285.2013.772929

Rossion, B., Collins, D., & Curran, T. (2007). Long-term expertise with artificial objects increases visual competition with early face categorization processes. *Journal of Cognitive Neurosciennce, 19*(3), 543–555. https://doi.org/10.1162/jocn.2007.19.3.543

Rossion, B. & Curran, T. (2010). Visual expertise with pictures of cars correlates with RT magnitude of the car inversion effect. *Perception, 39*(2). https://doi.org/10.1068/p6270

Rossion, B., Gauthier, I., Goffaux, V., Tarr, M. J., & Crommelinck, M. (2002). Expertise training with novel objects leads to left-lateralized facelike electrophysiological responses. *Psychological Science, 13*(3), 250–257. https://doi.org/10.1111/1467-9280.00446

Rossion, Bruno; Jacques, Corentin. The N170: understanding the time-course of face perception in the human brain. In: Steven J. Luck, *The Oxford Handbook of Event-Related Potential Components*, Oxford University Press: (United Kingdom) Oxford 2011, p. 115–142 http://hdl.handle.net/2078.1/110943 – DOI:10.1093/oxfordhb/9780195374148.013.0064

Rossion, B. & Pourtois, G. (2004). Revisiting Snodgrass and Vanderwart's object pictorial set: The role of surface detail in basic-level object recognition. *Perception, 33*(2), 217–236.

Schweinberger, S. R., Huddy, V., & Burton, A. M. (2004). N250r: A face-selective brain response to stimulus repetitions. *NeuroReport, 15*(9), 1501–1505.

Schyns, P. G. (1998). Diagnostic recognition: Task constraints, object information, and their interactions. *Cognition, 67*(1–2), 147–179.

Schyns, P. G. & Rodet, L. (1997). Categorization creates functional features. *Journal of Experimental Psychology: Learning, Memory and Cognition, 23*(3), 681–696.

Scolari, M., Vogel, E. K., & Awh, E. (2008). Perceptual expertise enhances the resolution but not the number of representations in working memory. *Psychonomic Bulletin and Review, 15*, 215–222.

Scott, L., Tanaka, J., Sheinberg, D., & Curran, T. (2006). A reevaluation of the electrophysiological correlates of expert object processing. *Journal of Cognitive Neuroscience, 18*(9), 1453–1465. https://doi.org/10.1162/jocn.2006.18.9.1453

Scott, L. S., Tanaka, J. W., Sheinberg, D. L., & Curran, T. (2008). The role of category learning in the acquisition and retention of perceptual expertise: A behavioral and neurophysiological study. *Brain Research*, *1210*, 204–215. https://doi.org/10.1016/j.brainres.2008.02.054

Shen, J., Mack, M. L., Palmeri, T. J., & Connors, M. H. (2014). Studying real-world perceptual expertise. *Frontiers in Psychology*, *5*, 857. https://doi .org/10.3389/fpsyg.2014.00857

Solomon, J. A. & Pelli, D. G. (1994). The visual filter mediating letter identification. *Nature*, *369*, 395–397. https://doi.org/10.1038/369395a0

Spence, C., Levitan, C. A., Shankar, M. U., & Zampini, M. (2010). Does food color influence taste and flavor perception in humans? *Chemosensory Perception*, *3*(1), 68–84. https://doi.org/10.1007/s12078-010-9067-z

Swensson, R. G. (1980). A 2-stage detection model applied to skilled visual-search by radiologists. *Perception and Psychophysics*, *27*(1), 11–16. https://doi.org/10.3758/BF03199899

Szegedy, C., Liu, W., Jia, Y. et al. (2014). Going deeper with convolutions: Technical report. *arXiv*. https://arxiv.org/abs/1409.4842

Tanaka, J. W. (2001). The entry point of face recognition. *Journal of Experimental Psychology: General*, *130*, 534–543.

Tanaka, J. W. & Curran, T. (2001). A neural basis for expert object recognition. *Psychological Science*, *12*(1), 43–47. https://doi.org/10.1111/1467-9280.00308.

Tanaka, J. W., Curran, T., Porterfield, A. L., & Collins, D. (2006). Activation of preexisting and acquired face representations: The N250 event-related potential as an index of face familiarity. *Journal of Cognitive Neuroscience*, *18*(9). https://doi.org/10.1162/jocn.2006.18.9.1488

Tanaka, J. W., Curran, T., & Sheinberg, D. (2005). The training and transfer of real-world perceptual expertise. *Psychological Science*, *16*(2), 145–151.

Tanaka, J. W. & Farah, M. J. (1993). Parts and wholes in face recognition. *The Quarterly Journal of Experimental Psychology Section A: Human Experimental Psychology*, *46*(2), 225–245.

Tanaka, J. W. & Pierce, L. J. (2009). The neural plasticity of other-race face recognition. *Cognitive, Affective and Behavioral Neuroscience*, *9*(1), 122–131.

Tanaka, J. W. & Presnell, L. M. (1999). Color diagnosticity in object recognition. *Perception and Psychophysics*, *61*(6), 1140–1153.

Tanaka, J. W. & Taylor, M. (1991). Object categories and expertise: Is the basic level in the eye of the beholder? *Cognitive Psychology*, *23*(3), 457–482. https://doi.org/10.1016/0010-0285(91)90016-H

Turner-Brown, L. M., Lam, K. S. L., Holtzclaw, T. N., Dichter, G. S., & Bodfish, J. W. (2011). Phenomenology and measurement of circumscribed interests in autism spectrum disorders. *Autism*, *15*(4), 437–456. https://doi.org/10.1177/1362361310386507

Tversky, B. (1989). Parts, partonomies, and taxonomies. *Developmental Psychology*, *25*(6), 983–995.

Tversky, B. & Hemenway, K. (1984). Objects, parts, and categories. *Journal of Experimental Psychology: General*, *113*, 169–193.

Ullman, S., Assif, L., Fetaya, E., & Harari, D. (2016). Atoms of recognition in human and computer vision. *Proceedings of the National Academy of Sciences of the United States of America*, *113*(10), 2744–2749.

Ventura, P., Fernandes, T., Leite, I., Almeida, V., Casqueiro, I., & Wong, A. (2017). The word-composite effect depends on abstract lexical representations but not surface features like case and font. *Frontiers in Perception Science*, *8*, 1036. https://doi.org/10.3389/fpsyg.2017.01036.

Ventura, P., Fernandes, T., Pereira, A. et al. (2020). Holistic word processing is correlated with efficiency in visual word recognition. *Attention, Perception, and Psychophysics*, *82*(5), 2739–2750. https://doi.org/10.3758/s13414-020-01988-2

Vogel, E. K., Woodman, G. F., & Luck, S. J. (2001). Storage of features, conjunctions, and objects in visual working memory. *Journal of Experimental Psychology: Human Perception and Performance*, *27*(1), 92–114. https://doi.org/10.1037/0096-1523.27.1.92

Waldrop, M. M. (2019). News feature: What are the limits of deep learning? *Proceedings of the National Academy of Sciences of the United States of America*, *116*(4),1074–1077.

Wang, L., Mottron, L., Peng, D., Berthiaume, C., & Dawson, M. (2007). Local bias and local-to-global interference without global deficit: A robust finding in autism under various conditions of attention, exposure time, and visual angle. *Cognitive Neuropsychology*, *24*(5), 550–574. https://doi.org/10.1080/13546800701417096

Wiese, Holger, Simone C. Tüttenberg, Brandon T. Ingram, Chelsea YX Chan, Zehra Gurbuz, A. Mike Burton, and Andrew W. Young. "A robust neural index of high face familiarity." *Psychological science* 30, no. 2 (2019): 261–272.

Winkler-Rhoades, N., Medin, D., Waxman, S. R., Woodring, J., & Ross, N. O. (2010). Naming the animals that come to mind: Effects of culture and experience on category fluency. *Journal of Cognition and Culture*, *10*(1–2), 205–220. https://doi.org/10.1163/156853710X497248

Wisniewski, E. J. & Murphy, G. L. (1989). Superordinate and basic category names in discourse: A textual analysis. *Discourse Processes.* https://doi.org/10.1080/01638538909544728

Wolfe, J. N. (1976). Risk for breast cancer development determined by mammographic parenchymal pattern. *Cancer, 37*(5), 2486–2492.

Wong, A. C.-N., Bukach, C. M., Yuen, C., Yang, L., Leung, S., & Greenspon, E. (2011). Holistic processing of words modulated by reading experience. *PloS One, 6*(6), e20753. https://doi.org/10.1371/journal.pone.0020753

Wong, A. C.-N., Palmeri, T. J., & Gauthier, I. (2009). Conditions for facelike expertise with objects: Becoming a ziggerin expert – but which type? *Psychological Science, 20*(9), 1108–1117. https://doi.org/10.1111/j.1467-9280.2009.02430.x

Wong, Y. K., & Gauthier, I. (2010). Holistic processing of musical notation: Dissociating failures of selective attention in experts and novices. *Cognitive, Affective, & Behavioral Neuroscience, 10*(4), 541–551. https://doi.org/10.3758/CABN.10.4.541

Wurm, L. H., Legge, G. E., Isenberg, L. M., & Luebker, A. (1993). Color improves object recognition in normal and low vision. *Journal of Experimental Psychology: Human perception and performance, 19(4)*, 899.

Xu, B., Rourke, L., Robinson, J. K., & Tanaka, J. W. (2016). Training melanoma detection in photographs using the perceptual expertise training approach. *Applied Cognitive Psychology, 30*(5), 750–756.

Xu, Y. (2005). Revisiting the role of the fusiform face area in visual expertise. *Cerebral Cortex. 15*(8), 1234–1242. https://doi.org/10.1093/cercor/bhi006

Yamins, D. L. K., Hong, H., Cadieu, C. F., Solomon, E. A., Seibert, D., & DiCarlo, J. J. (2014). Performance-optimized hierarchical models predict neural responses in higher visual cortex. *Proceedings of the National Academy of Sciences, 111*(23), 8619–8624.

Yin, R. K. (1969). Looking at upside-down faces. *Journal of experimental psychology, 81*(1), 141.

Young, A. W., Hellawell, D., & Hay, D. C. (2013). Configurational information in face perception. *Perception, 42*(11), 1166–1178.

## Cambridge Elements ≡

# Perception

### James T. Enns
*The University of British Columbia*

Editor James T. Enns is Professor at the University of British Columbia, where he researches the interaction of perception, attention, emotion, and social factors. He has previously been Editor of the *Journal of Experimental Psychology: Human Perception and Performance* and an Associate Editor at *Psychological Science, Consciousness and Cognition, Attention Perception & Psychophysics,* and *Visual Cognition.*

### Editorial Board

### About the Series

The modern study of human perception includes event perception, bidirectional influences between perception and action, music, language, the integration of the senses, human action observation, and the important roles of emotion, motivation, and social factors. Each Element in the series combines authoritative literature reviews of foundational topics with forward-looking presentations of the recent developments on a given topic.

# Cambridge Elements ≡

## Perception

Printed in the United States
by Baker & Taylor Publisher Services